The Enneagram and Money

Bradley Hall

Published by Defenestration Press, 2023.

While every precaution has been taken in the preparation of this book, the publisher assumes no responsibility for errors or omissions, or for damages resulting from the use of the information contained herein.

THE ENNEAGRAM AND MONEY

First edition. September 2, 2023.

ISBN: 979-8860049673

Written by Bradley Hall.

Table of Contents

Chapter 1: Unveiling the Enneagram's Impact on Our Financial Dynamics 1

Chapter 2: The Perfectionist (Type 1) 22

Chapter 3: The Helper (Type 2) 38

Chapter 4: The Achiever (Type 3) 56

Chapter 5: The Individualist (Type 4) 70

Chapter 6: The Investigator (Type 5) 84

Chapter 7: The Loyalist (Type 6) 99

Chapter 8: The Enthusiast (Type 7) 115

Chapter 9: The Challenger (Type 8) 132

Chapter 10: The Peacemaker (Type 9) 150

Chapter 11: The Effect of Wings 163

Chapter 12: Other Things to Know 180

Introduction

Have you ever wondered why money has such a powerful hold on our lives? Why does it dictate our every decision, our every thought, our every action? Is it merely the means to survival, or is there something deeper at play? These questions have plagued me for years, leading me on a journey of exploration and self-discovery. And now, dear reader, I invite you to join me as they dive into the fascinating world of the Enneagram and its intricate relationship with money.

In a world where the pursuit of wealth and success seems to overshadow all else, it is essential to examine the underlying motivations that drive our actions. The Enneagram, a powerful system of personality typing, offers profound insights into our deepest fears, desires, and needs. It uncovers the complex web of emotions and beliefs that underpin our relationship with money. From the driven Type Three, seeking validation through material success, to the innovative and visionary Type Five, who values knowledge over material wealth, the Enneagram shines a light on our true selves in relation to money.

Our modern society teaches us that money equals happiness, success, and power. It promises fulfillment and security, pulling us into an endless cycle of acquisition and consumption. But as our bank accounts swell, so too does our discontent. They find themselves trapped in a never-ending pursuit of more, never realizing that true abundance lies not in our possessions but in our connection to ourselves and others.

To allay their financial fears and anxieties, most people follow the traditional path of accumulating wealth, chasing promotions, and sacrificing their wellbeing in the name of success. They cling to the belief that happiness can be bought, that money will solve all their problems. But all too often, they find themselves disillusioned, empty, and yearning for more.

The Enneagram and Money presents a groundbreaking approach to understanding our relationship with wealth and abundance. By delving deep into the nine types of the Enneagram and examining their unique perspectives, fears, and motivations, they gain invaluable insights into our own financial patterns and habits. This book offers a roadmap towards true financial freedom, one rooted in self-awareness and self-compassion.

Dear reader, you have likely felt the weight of financial expectations pressing down upon your shoulders. The relentless pursuit of money has left you feeling disconnected from your true self, your passions, and your purpose. But fear not, for within these pages, they will embark on a transformative journey— a journey that will not only change your relationship with money but also transform your entire approach to life.

Imagine a world where money is no longer a source of stress and anxiety, where your worth is not measured by your bank balance but by the love and joy that fills your heart. Envision a future where you wake up every day excited to follow your passions and make a meaningful impact in the world. Together, they can bring this vision to life.

Welcome to The Enneagram and Money, a book that will challenge your beliefs, ignite your curiosity, and empower you to reclaim your financial story. Through a captivating exploration of the Enneagram, they will unlock the secrets of your type's unique relationship with money and guide you towards a life of abundance, fulfillment, and true health. Buckle up, dear reader, for this journey will be like no other. Together, they will embark on a transformational odyssey that will forever change the way you view money and your place in the world. Are you ready to delve into the depths of your Enneagram type and uncover the hidden truths that lie within? Then join me as they embark on this extraordinary adventure into the heart and soul of the Enneagram and its enthralling connection with money.

Chapter 1: Unveiling the Enneagram's Impact on Our Financial Dynamics

What Is the Enneagram?

The Enneagram system is a profound and intricate framework that offers deep insights into the human psyche and our patterns of behavior. Rooted in ancient wisdom and teachings, the Enneagram has gained immense popularity in recent years as a tool for self-discovery, personal growth, and transformation.

At its core, the Enneagram is a personality typing system that outlines nine distinct personality types, each with its own set of characteristics, tendencies, and core motivations. These types are represented by nine points on a circle, creating a visual representation of the interconnectedness of the human experience. Each personality type is influenced by adjacent types, indicating that our behaviors and qualities are not fixed but rather shaped by a combination of influences.

The Enneagram serves as a powerful tool for self-awareness. By identifying our Enneagram type and studying its underlying motivations, fears, and desires, they can gain a deeper understanding of ourselves and our patterns of behavior. This profound self-awareness provides a framework for personal growth and transformation, helping us move beyond our limitations, challenges, and self-imposed barriers.

Let me briefly introduce you to the nine personality types within the Enneagram system:

Type 1, known as the Perfectionist, is driven by a strong sense of responsibility and a desire for order and perfection.

Type 2, the Helper, is characterized by their nurturing nature and their tendency to prioritize others' needs over their own.

Type 3, the Achiever, is goal-oriented and ambitious, constantly striving for success and recognition.

Type 4, the Individualist, is deeply in touch with their emotions and focuses on their personal identity and creative self-expression.

Type 5, the Investigator, is curious and analytical, preferring solitude and intellectual pursuits.

Type 6, the Loyalist, is loyal and cautious, seeking guidance and reassurance in the face of potential threats.

Type 7, the Enthusiast, is optimistic and adventurous, constantly seeking stimulation and avoiding discomfort.

Type 8, the Challenger, is assertive and focused on personal power and justice.

Type 9, the Peacemaker, desires inner and outer peace, often avoiding conflict and seeking harmony and stability.

Understanding these nine types provides a framework for exploring our unique relationship with money. Each type has its own lens through which it views wealth, abundance, and financial security. By delving into the Enneagram and examining our own Type's perspective, they can uncover the hidden beliefs, fears, and motivations that influence our financial patterns and habits.

Dear reader, together they will embark on a transformative journey—a journey that will not only change your relationship with money but also transform your entire approach to life. Imagine a world where money is no longer a source of stress and anxiety, where your worth is not measured by your bank balance but by the love and joy that fills your heart.

So, let us dive deep into the Enneagram and unlock the secrets of your type's unique relationship with money. Brace yourself, for this journey will be like no other—a transformational odyssey that will forever change the way you view money and your place in the world. Together, they can create a future where financial freedom is not just a dream but a tangible reality. Are you ready to embark on this extraordinary adventure?

Why Explore the Enneagram and Money?

Why should they explore the Enneagram and its relationship with money? This question has been asked countless times, and yet the answers continue to be as vast and profound as the human experience itself. To truly understand the significance of this exploration, they must first recognize the Enneagram as a powerful tool for self-discovery and understanding.

The Enneagram, with its nine distinct personality types, unveils the complexity and diversity of human nature. Each type brings its own set of financial behaviors and beliefs to the table, creating a kaleidoscope of financial experiences. Type 1, the Perfectionist, is diligent and conscientious, often striving for financial stability and security. Type 2, the Helper, is generous and giving, placing a great deal of importance on financial support and assistance. Type 3, the Achiever, is driven and success-oriented, valuing financial accomplishments as a measure of self-worth. Type 4, the Individualist, seeks uniqueness and authenticity, often attaching emotional significance to money and possessions. Type 5, the Investigator, is curious and independent, approaching finances with a cautious and analytical mindset. Type 6, the Loyalist, is loyal and security-seeking, making financial decisions based on a need for stability and certainty. Type 7, the Enthusiast, is adventurous and optimistic, often viewing money as a means to enjoy life and experience new things. Excited by possibilities, Type 7s may be prone to impulse spending on activities or items that promise immediate enjoyment or gratification. Type 8, the Challenger, is assertive and confident, often taking a direct and confrontational approach to managing their finances. For Type 8s, money is often seen as a tool for independence and control over their environment. Type 9, the Peacemaker, seeks harmony and avoids conflict, which can sometimes extend to their financial lives as well.

Understanding our financial behaviors and beliefs is crucial for personal and financial growth. By exploring the Enneagram and its connection to money, they open themselves up to a journey of self-awareness and transformation. They gain insight into the root causes of our financial patterns and challenges, understanding how our personality type influences our attitudes towards money, spending habits, and attitudes towards wealth. Armed with this knowledge, they can begin to align our financial behaviors with our true selves, moving towards a more harmonious and fulfilling relationship with money.

The benefits of exploring the Enneagram and money are manifold. Self-awareness can lead to healthier financial behaviors, improved decision-making, and enhanced financial well-being. By examining our relationship with material possessions, they can gain insights into our values and priorities, fostering a sense of contentment and fulfillment that extends far beyond monetary measures. Understanding our motivations behind financial choices allows us to make conscious and intentional decisions, freeing ourselves from the constraints of unconscious spending or hoarding. Moreover, exploring the Enneagram and money provides a roadmap for personal growth and development. they can identify areas of strength and areas in need of growth, embracing the opportunity to expand our financial consciousness and capability.

This exploration also deepens our understanding of ourselves and others. By delving into the Enneagram and its connection to money, they cultivate empathy and compassion in our financial interactions. they become more aware of the diverse financial perspectives and challenges faced by individuals of different types. This awareness allows us to build more meaningful and authentic relationships, fostering a sense of support and unity that transcends financial divides.

In the upcoming chapters of this book, they will dive into each Enneagram type's financial mindset and behaviors, shedding light on the intricacies of their relationship with money. You will discover the nuances of your own financial tendencies and the deep-seated beliefs that drive them. Through these revelations, they will provide practical strategies, insights, and guidance for each type to achieve a more balanced and fulfilling financial life. This book is not just a theoretical exploration; it is meant to support you in aligning your financial behaviors with your true self, empowering you to create a life of abundance and authenticity.

Reflect on the importance of exploring the Enneagram and money. This undertaking holds the promise of personal growth, financial well-being, and a profound shift in your relationship with money. It is an opportunity to uncover the hidden layers of your financial story and embrace a future where money is no longer a source of stress and anxiety, but a tool for creating the life you desire. I encourage you to embark on this extraordinary adventure with me for the journey ahead will undoubtedly transform the way you view money and your place in the world. Together, they will unlock the secrets of the Enneagram and money, revealing a path to abundance, fulfillment, and true wealth. Are you ready to take the plunge?

Benefits of Understanding the Enneagram and Money

Understanding the Enneagram and its relationship with money holds immense potential for our financial well-being. As a finance expert deeply interested in the Enneagram, I have witnessed how this powerful tool can provide valuable insights into our financial mindset and behaviors. By unraveling the underlying motivations, fears, and patterns associated with each Enneagram type, they can uncover a wealth of knowledge that can transform our financial lives. In this segment, they will explore the numerous benefits of understanding the Enneagram and money, diving deep into each aspect to illuminate the path to financial success and fulfillment.

One of the key benefits of understanding the Enneagram's connection to money is the development of financial self-awareness. The Enneagram helps us delve into our own motivations, attitudes, and behaviors when it comes to finances, allowing us to gain a deeper understanding of ourselves. By becoming more aware of our financial triggers, desires, and fears, they can make conscious and intentional financial decisions that align with our values and goals. This self-awareness becomes the foundation for building a healthy and prosperous financial life.

Knowledge of our Enneagram type offers a powerful tool for identifying and breaking detrimental financial patterns. They all have patterns and habits that hold us back financially, whether it's impulsive spending, excessive worry about money, or a lack of long-term financial planning. By understanding the motivations behind these patterns, they can free themselves from self-sabotaging behaviors and adopt new, more beneficial financial choices. The Enneagram acts as a mirror that reflects our deepest insecurities and shows us the path towards healthier financial habits.

The Enneagram not only offers insights into our own financial behaviors but also provides a framework for understanding the financial behaviors of others. By understanding the Enneagram types of those they interact with, whether family, friends, or colleagues, they can improve our communication, collaboration, and mutual understanding when it comes to money matters. This understanding can dissolve conflicts, foster empathy, and pave the way for more harmonious financial relationships. Together, they can create a supportive and inclusive financial environment, where everyone's unique perspectives and needs are acknowledged and valued.

In pursuit of financial well-being, finding balance is crucial. The Enneagram dives deep into our tendencies towards financial extremes, such as overspending or extreme frugality, and provides strategies for achieving a more balanced approach. By understanding our Enneagram type, they can recognize our inherent strengths and areas for growth when it comes to finance. With this knowledge, they can develop strategies to harness our strengths while tempering our tendencies towards financial imbalances. This newfound balance allows us to make sound decisions, invest wisely, and live a fulfilling financial life.

THE ENNEAGRAM AND MONEY

Fear and anxiety often underpin our financial decisions and behaviors, holding us back from financial growth and fulfillment. The Enneagram provides a roadmap for understanding these fears by delving into the underlying motivations and anxieties associated with each Enneagram type. Armed with this knowledge, they can develop the courage to confront our financial fears head-on. They can shift our relationship with money from one of fear and scarcity to one of empowerment and abundance. The Enneagram gives us the tools to transform our financial mindset and build a foundation of confidence and resilience.

Understanding our Enneagram type not only sheds light on our challenges but also helps us identify and leverage our unique strengths in pursuit of financial success. The Enneagram reveals our natural talents, abilities, and perspectives, which they can leverage to maximize our potential in professional and financial endeavors. By understanding and harnessing these strengths, they can approach financial opportunities with confidence and navigate challenges with agility. The Enneagram becomes a guiding compass that leads us towards our true financial strengths and empowers us to pursue our financial goals with purpose and authenticity.

Building financial resilience is essential in today's ever-changing economic landscape. The Enneagram, with its deep insights into our coping mechanisms and reactions to adversity, can help us develop this crucial trait. By understanding our Enneagram type, they can become more aware of our instinctive responses to financial challenges, be they avoidance, aggression, or passivity. Armed with this knowledge, they can cultivate healthier coping strategies and build financial resilience. The Enneagram transforms setbacks into opportunities for growth, ensuring that they can weather financial storms and emerge stronger on the other side.

Our financial choices have a profound impact on our lives and the world around us. By understanding our Enneagram type, they gain clarity on what truly matters to us, enabling us to align our financial decisions with our deepest values. The Enneagram helps us prioritize our financial goals, ensure our spending aligns with our values, and direct our financial resources towards creating a meaningful impact. It allows us to cultivate financial integrity, where our money becomes a tool for creating the life they desire while promoting the greater good.

Ultimately, the Enneagram's profound understanding of our unique motivations, desires, and fears leads to increased financial satisfaction and fulfillment. By embracing our Enneagram type, they embark on a journey of self-acceptance and self-compassion. This self-awareness brings contentment and joy that extends far beyond monetary measures. they learn to redefine what financial success means to us, embracing a path that aligns with our authentic selves. The Enneagram invites us to find satisfaction in balancing our financial resources, pursuing our passions, and living a life infused with purpose.

The Enneagram has the remarkable ability to shift our financial mindset from one of scarcity to one of abundance. Through understanding our Enneagram type, they uncover our limiting beliefs and fears that keep us trapped in a scarcity mindset. Armed with this knowledge, they can transform our relationship with money, cultivating a sense of gratitude, openness, and abundance. The Enneagram allows us to embrace the inherent abundance in our financial lives, recognizing the opportunities and possibilities that exist beyond our perceived limitations. With this perspective, they can attract and manifest greater financial abundance.

As they conclude this segment on the benefits of understanding the Enneagram and money, I invite you to reflect on the tremendous potential for personal and financial growth that lies ahead. The Enneagram offers a holistic framework for transforming our financial lives, enabling us to create abundance and authenticity. In the subsequent chapters of this book, they will delve deep into each Enneagram type's financial mindset and behaviors, providing practical strategies, insights, and guidance tailored to your unique type. I encourage you to embrace this extraordinary adventure of self-discovery and financial empowerment. Together, they will unlock the secrets of the Enneagram and money, paving the way towards a life of abundance, fulfillment, and true wealth. Are you ready to take the plunge?

How to Use This Book

Welcome to "The Enneagram and Money"! In this segment, they will provide you with guidance on how to effectively use the information provided in this book for your personal growth and financial transformation. Understanding the

Enneagram and its relationship with money is just the first step towards achieving financial abundance and fulfillment. Let's dive in and explore how you can make the most out of this book.

Start by reading the introduction to get a clear overview of the Enneagram and its significance in understanding our relationship with money. This will lay the foundation for the chapters that follow and give you valuable insights into why certain financial patterns and behaviors emerge based on the different Enneagram types.

After exploring the general impact of the Enneagram on our financial lives, it's time to delve into the specifics of each Enneagram type. Each chapter is devoted to exploring the financial mindset and behaviors of a specific type, providing actionable guidance for creating a healthier and more balanced financial life.

As you read through each chapter, take notes and reflect on how the information resonates with your own financial experiences. The Enneagram is a powerful tool for self-reflection, and understanding your Enneagram type can be a catalyst for personal growth and transformation. Even reading the chapters that are not of your type will help you learn more about the people and the world around you and their views on money and finance.

Pay particular attention to the subchapters within each type chapter. These subchapters address specific aspects of each Enneagram type's financial patterns and challenges, offering tailored insights and strategies for overcoming obstacles and aligning your financial behaviors with your personal values.

Don't forget to explore Chapter 11, where they delve into the effects of wings. Understanding the influence of your wing on your financial behaviors can provide additional clarity and depth to your self-discovery journey, uncovering hidden strengths and potential blind spots.

Once you have absorbed the core content of the book, turn your attention to Chapter 12, "Other Things to Know." This chapter addresses additional aspects and considerations related to the Enneagram and money that can further enhance your understanding and application. From exploring the impact of childhood experiences on your financial mindset to discovering the importance of self-compassion in your financial journey, this chapter will provide valuable insights beyond the Enneagram types.

Finally, as you navigate through the book, take the time to reflect on your own financial journey and how the insights from each chapter apply to your unique circumstances. Ask yourself thought-provoking questions, journal your thoughts, and consider seeking support from professionals or joining Enneagram and money discussion groups to deepen your understanding and further accelerate your personal and financial growth.

Remember, "The Enneagram and Money" is not just a book to be read, but a transformative tool to help you unlock your financial potential and create a life of abundance and fulfillment. Embrace this journey, and may it bring you profound insights and lasting change.

Enneagram types of those they interact with, whether family, friends, or colleagues, can improve our communication, collaboration, and mutual understanding when it comes to money matters. This understanding can dissolve conflicts, foster empathy, and pave the way for more harmonious financial relationships. Together, they can create a supportive and inclusive financial environment, where everyone's unique perspectives and needs are acknowledged and valued.

Finding balance is crucial in pursuit of financial well-being. The Enneagram dives deep into our tendencies towards financial extremes, such as overspending or extreme frugality, and provides strategies for achieving a more balanced approach. By understanding our Enneagram type, they can recognize our inherent strengths and areas for growth when it comes to finance. With this knowledge, they can develop strategies to harness our strengths while tempering our tendencies towards financial imbalances. This newfound balance allows us to make sound decisions, invest wisely, and live a fulfilling financial life.

Fear and anxiety often underpin our financial decisions and behaviors, holding us back from financial growth and fulfillment. The Enneagram provides a roadmap for understanding these fears by delving into the underlying motivations and anxieties associated with each Enneagram type. Armed with this knowledge, they can develop the courage to confront our financial fears head-on. They can shift our relationship with money from one of fear and scarcity to one of empowerment and abundance. The Enneagram gives us the tools to transform our financial mindset and build a foundation of confidence and resilience.

Understanding our Enneagram type not only sheds light on our challenges but also helps us identify and leverage our unique strengths in pursuit of financial success. The Enneagram reveals our natural talents, abilities, and perspectives, which they can leverage to maximize our potential in professional and financial endeavors. By understanding and harnessing these strengths, they can approach financial opportunities with confidence and navigate challenges with agility. The Enneagram becomes a guiding compass that leads us towards our true financial strengths and empowers us to pursue our financial goals with purpose and authenticity.

Building financial resilience is essential in today's ever-changing economic landscape. The Enneagram, with its deep insights into our coping mechanisms and reactions to adversity, can help us develop this crucial trait. By understanding our Enneagram type, they can become more aware of our instinctive responses to financial challenges, be they avoidance, aggression, or passivity. Armed with this knowledge, they can cultivate healthier coping strategies and build financial resilience. The Enneagram transforms setbacks into opportunities for growth, ensuring that they can weather financial storms and emerge stronger on the other side.

Our financial choices have a profound impact on our lives and the world around us. By understanding our Enneagram type, they gain clarity on what truly matters to us, enabling us to align our financial decisions with our deepest values. The Enneagram helps us prioritize our financial goals, ensure our spending aligns with our values, and direct our financial resources towards creating a meaningful impact. It allows us to cultivate financial integrity, where our money becomes a tool for creating the life they desire while promoting the greater good.

Ultimately, the Enneagram's profound understanding of our unique motivations, desires, and fears leads to increased financial satisfaction and fulfillment. By embracing our Enneagram type, they embark on a journey of self-acceptance and self-compassion. This self-awareness brings contentment and joy that extends far beyond monetary measures. they learn to redefine what financial success means to us, embracing a path that aligns with our authentic selves. The Enneagram invites us to find satisfaction in balancing our financial resources, pursuing our passions, and living a life infused with purpose.

The Enneagram has the remarkable ability to shift our financial mindset from one of scarcity to one of abundance. Through understanding our Enneagram type, they uncover our limiting beliefs and fears that keep us trapped in a scarcity mindset. Armed with this knowledge, they can transform our relationship with money, cultivating a sense of gratitude, openness, and abundance. The Enneagram allows us to embrace the inherent abundance in our financial lives, recognizing the opportunities and possibilities that exist beyond our perceived limitations. With this perspective, they can attract and manifest greater financial abundance.

As they conclude this segment on the benefits of understanding the Enneagram and money, I invite you to reflect on the tremendous potential for personal and financial growth that lies ahead. The Enneagram offers a holistic framework for transforming our financial lives, enabling us to create abundance and authenticity. In the subsequent chapters of this book, they will delve deep into each Enneagram type's financial mindset and behaviors, providing practical strategies, insights, and guidance tailored to your unique type. I encourage you to embrace this extraordinary adventure of self-discovery and financial empowerment. Together, they will unlock the secrets of the Enneagram and money, paving the way towards a life of abundance, fulfillment, and true wealth. Are you ready to take the plunge?

Disclaimer

As they continue on this transformative journey exploring the intricate relationship between the Enneagram and money, it is important to set a clear context for the content that lies ahead. The Enneagram is a powerful tool for self-discovery and personal growth, offering profound insights into our motivations, fears, and desires. In the context of finance, it can help us uncover the underlying patterns and behaviors that influence our financial decisions – from our spending habits to our attitude towards wealth. However, it is essential to establish that the information provided in this book is not intended to be financial advice. Understanding this distinction is crucial to ensuring that readers approach the content with the right mindset and seek professional guidance for their financial needs.

I want to make it explicit that the content presented in "The Enneagram and Money" is not meant to replace professional financial advice. While I am a finance expert with a deep interest in the Enneagram's intersection with money, it is imperative to acknowledge that every individual's financial circumstances are unique. Therefore, it is crucial that readers consult with qualified financial advisors for personalized guidance tailored to their specific situations. The information provided in this book serves as a tool to enhance self-awareness and understanding of money patterns, but it should not be taken as specific financial advice.

The core focus of this book is on self-awareness and introspection. By exploring the connections between the Enneagram and our relationship with money, my aim is to help readers gain deep insight into their own money patterns and behaviors. The power of self-awareness cannot be overstated, especially when it comes to financial decision-making. By examining our inner motivations and unconscious biases, they can make more conscious choices that align with our values and lead to greater financial well-being. Through self-awareness, they have the opportunity to uncover ingrained money patterns and transform them into healthier, more fulfilling behaviors.

THE ENNEAGRAM AND MONEY

One of the key objectives of this book is to shed light on the importance of understanding our money patterns. Our financial behaviors are often driven by deeply ingrained patterns that are influenced by our Enneagram types and personal histories. By delving into these patterns, they can gain valuable insights into our relationship with money and the ways in which it may be impacting our lives. Whether it is recognizing self-sabotaging behaviors or understanding the push and pull between accumulation and generosity, understanding our money patterns is a crucial step towards personal growth and financial success.

It is important to clarify the scope of this book and manage expectations accordingly. While it delves deep into the fascinating connection between the Enneagram and money, it does not provide specific investment advice or financial planning tips. Rather, the purpose of this book is to guide readers in exploring their relationship with money from a psychological perspective. By understanding the motivations and behaviors that are rooted in our Enneagram types, readers can equip themselves with the knowledge needed to make more informed financial decisions aligned with their authentic selves.

I cannot stress enough the importance of seeking professional financial advice when it comes to specific financial matters such as investments, debt management, tax planning, and the like. While this book will undoubtedly provide valuable insights and strategies for personal growth, it should never be a substitute for the personalized advice of qualified professionals. I encourage readers to use the knowledge gained from this book as a foundation for meaningful discussions with their financial advisors. Synergizing self-awareness and professional financial guidance can set the stage for holistic financial success and personal fulfillment.

Throughout this book, I provide practical exercises and tools for self-reflection and personal growth. These exercises are meant to deepen the reader's understanding of their money patterns and offer insights into potential areas for growth. However, it is important to note that these exercises are not intended to offer financial recommendations. Instead, they are designed to facilitate self-discovery and empower readers to take ownership of their financial journey. By engaging with these tools, readers can begin to transform their relationship with money and create a life of abundance and fulfillment.

As with any book or source of information, readers have a responsibility to critically evaluate and apply the concepts and strategies outlined in their own lives. The Enneagram and its insights into our financial behaviors and patterns are not one-size-fits-all solutions. Each individual's experiences and circumstances are unique, and therefore, their own judgment is essential in applying the content of this book. It is vital to adapt the information to one's personal situation, and consider seeking further professional advice where necessary.

As they come to the end of this disclaimer, I want to express my utmost gratitude for embarking on this transformative adventure with me. "The Enneagram and Money" is not just a book; it is a tool for unlocking your financial potential and creating a life of abundance and fulfillment. Embrace this journey of self-discovery, and may it bring you profound insights and lasting change. Remember, true wealth goes beyond mere monetary measures, and through the Enneagram, they have the opportunity to redefine financial success and live a life infused with purpose and authenticity. Now, let us turn the page together and continue on this extraordinary path of self and financial empowerment.

Chapter 2: The Perfectionist (Type 1)

The Perfectionist's Relationship With Money

Perfectionism plays a significant role in Type 1's financial choices. They hold themselves to high standards when it comes to money management and financial goals. Their meticulous attention to detail and desire for excellence push them to pursue financial success with unwavering determination. However, this constant pursuit of perfection can sometimes hinder their ability to make practical financial decisions.

One of the core fears that drives Type 1's financial decisions is the fear of making mistakes. They seek to avoid any missteps that could compromise their financial security or integrity. This fear can lead to cautious and conservative behavior, such as avoiding risks or excessive saving. However, it is important for Type 1 individuals to find a balance between their pursuit of perfection and the practicality required in making sound financial choices.

Seeking security and stability is a fundamental motivation for Type 1 individuals in their financial lives. They value having a solid financial foundation and often exhibit responsible habits, such as budgeting and avoiding debt. While this drive for security is commendable, an excessive focus on it can hinder their willingness to invest or take calculated financial risks.

Finding the right balance between security and growth is crucial for Type 1's financial well-being.

Type 1 individuals have a natural propensity to strive for perfection in their financial endeavors. They meticulously create budgets, track expenses, and set rigid financial goals. While this dedication to detail can help them achieve their financial targets, it is important for them to balance this pursuit of perfection with self-compassion and flexibility. Recognizing that imperfections are part of the financial journey and embracing adaptability is key for Type 1 individuals to find fulfillment and peace with their financial outcomes.

To overcome their fear of financial failure, Type 1 individuals can adopt strategies that embrace growth and learning from mistakes. It is crucial for them to accept that financial success is not achieved without setbacks along the way. By cultivating a growth mindset and viewing mistakes as stepping stones towards improvement, Type 1 individuals can navigate their fear of failure and transform it into opportunities for personal growth and financial resilience.

Type 1 individuals place great importance on adhering to personal values and principles. This strong sense of ethics and integrity can guide their financial choices. However, it is essential for them to find a balance between rigid adherence to personal values and the need for flexibility in financial decisions. Understanding that financial circumstances may change and adapting without compromising core values can help Type 1 individuals navigate the challenges they may encounter on their financial journey.

For Type 1 individuals, finding balance and contentment in their financial lives while managing their perfectionistic tendencies can be a challenge. Setting realistic expectations and embracing imperfections are key to achieving this balance. By cultivating self-acceptance and gratitude for their financial achievements, Type 1 individuals can experience a sense of fulfillment regardless of reaching their ideals. It is crucial for them to understand that financial well-being is not solely measured by external factors but also by finding peace within themselves.

To aid in their financial growth, Type 1 individuals can benefit from seeking professional financial guidance. A financial advisor or planner who understands and respects their personality traits and financial goals can provide objective insights and strategies to navigate their perfectionistic tendencies. Collaborating with a trusted professional can offer guidance and support in managing their finances, while also ensuring their holistic well-being is taken into account.

Type 1 individuals can utilize their financial experiences as opportunities for personal growth. By embracing vulnerability, adaptability, and self-reflection, they can further develop their character and values through their financial decision-making. Recognizing that mistakes are inevitable and using them as catalysts for growth, Type 1 individuals can enhance their self-awareness, resilience, and overall well-being.

Understanding the perfectionist's relationship with money is crucial for Type 1 individuals to navigate their financial journey with wisdom and self-compassion. By acknowledging and managing their core motivations and fears, they can find balance, fulfillment, and growth. Embracing self-awareness and self-compassion while aligning financial decisions with personal values empower Type 1 individuals to create a financially secure and fulfilling life. May this understanding open doors to greater financial empowerment and personal development.

Financial Challenges Faced by Type 1

Type 1 individuals, known as the Perfectionists, face a unique set of financial challenges due to their innate desire for order, structure, and perfection. Their meticulous attention to detail and unwavering commitment to doing things right can sometimes hinder their financial progress and cause undue stress. It is essential for Type 1 individuals to understand these challenges and develop strategies to overcome them in order to achieve financial success and peace of mind.

One of the primary challenges faced by Type 1 individuals is their tendency to prioritize financial stability and security above all else. Their fear of making mistakes or jeopardizing their financial well-being often leads them to adopt a conservative approach to money management. While this caution can be beneficial in some instances, it can also restrict them from taking calculated risks or seizing potentially lucrative opportunities. Type 1 individuals need to find a balance between striving for stability and allowing themselves to take calculated risks that can lead to financial growth and opportunities.

Another challenge that Type 1 individuals often encounter is the tendency to overanalyze financial decisions. Their desire to make the perfect choice can result in hesitancy and missed opportunities. Type 1 individuals may find themselves caught in a cycle of analysis paralysis, constantly second-guessing their financial choices and delaying action. It is essential for them to recognize that perfection is unattainable and that taking decisive action, even if it is not perfect, is often more productive than inaction.

Self-criticism and guilt are emotions that Type 1 individuals frequently experience when it comes to their financial choices. The fear of making financial mistakes or not meeting their own high standards can lead to harsh self-judgment and a constant sense of dissatisfaction. Type 1 individuals must develop strategies to manage and mitigate these self-critical thoughts and emotions. Practicing self-compassion and accepting that financial imperfections are a natural part of life can help alleviate these feelings and promote a healthier relationship with money.

Finding a balance between responsible budgeting and allowing themselves to enjoy their money is another challenge Type 1 individuals often face. They may be inclined to restrict their spending and deny themselves pleasures in order to maintain financial security and adhere to their perfectionistic tendencies. However, it is vital for Type 1 individuals to recognize the importance of enjoying the fruits of their labor and allowing themselves to indulge in experiences that bring them joy and fulfillment. This balance between responsible budgeting and enjoying their money is essential for maintaining long-term financial well-being and overall life satisfaction.

Investment decisions can also pose a challenge to Type 1 individuals. Their fear of making mistakes or not finding the perfect investment opportunity can lead to hesitation and missed opportunities for growth. Type 1 individuals must overcome their perfectionistic tendencies when it comes to investments and learn to accept that some level of risk is inherent in the investment process. Seeking professional advice and guidance from trusted financial advisors can help Type 1 individuals navigate this challenge and make informed investment decisions that align with their long-term financial goals.

Flexibility is another crucial aspect that Type 1 individuals need to embrace in order to overcome their financial challenges. Life is unpredictable, and unexpected circumstances can disrupt even the most carefully crafted financial plans. Type 1 individuals must learn to adjust their plans and strategies when needed, rather than rigidly holding onto a predefined path. Embracing flexibility allows them to adapt to changing circumstances and make the necessary financial adjustments to maintain stability and progress towards their goals.

In order to overcome these challenges, Type 1 individuals might benefit from seeking professional financial guidance. By collaborating with a trusted financial advisor who understands their personality traits, values, and goals, Type 1 individuals can receive objective insights and strategies to effectively manage their finances. The guidance of a professional can alleviate some of the burden of decision-making and provide the support needed to navigate their perfectionistic tendencies and achieve financial success.

Ultimately, Type 1 individuals must embrace the idea of imperfection in their financial lives. Accepting that mistakes and setbacks are inevitable allows them to let go of the need for perfection and find contentment in their financial outcomes. By cultivating self-awareness, practicing self-compassion, and setting realistic goals, Type 1 individuals can overcome their perfectionistic tendencies and pave the way for personal growth and financial empowerment. Letting go of the fear of failure and embracing the lessons that can be learned from mistakes, Type 1 individuals can transform their relationship with money and find fulfillment in the journey of building wealth.

Harnessing the Strengths of Type 1 for Financial Success

In harnessing the strengths of Type 1 for financial success, it is crucial to understand the core characteristics of the Perfectionist and how they relate to money. Type 1 individuals are driven by a strong sense of responsibility and hold themselves to high standards. They have a natural inclination towards prudence and discernment, paying attention to even the smallest of details. They are goal-oriented, thorough, self-disciplined, and value integrity and ethical behavior.

The strength of responsibility is a key attribute of Type 1 individuals that can be channeled into financial planning and goal setting. They excel in managing their finances responsibly, ensuring that their financial decisions align with their values and long-term objectives. Type 1 individuals take charge of their financial future by diligently tracking and managing their expenses, planning for emergencies, and setting clear financial goals. By taking responsibility for their financial well-being, they create a solid foundation for their future success.

Prudence and discernment are qualities that Type 1 individuals naturally possess. They have an innate ability to make sound financial decisions and avoid unnecessary risks. Their strong sense of discernment allows them to evaluate potential investments or financial opportunities with a critical eye, ensuring that they align with their overall financial objectives. This makes them well-positioned to build a secure and stable financial future.

One of the hallmarks of Type 1 individuals is their attention to detail. They leave no stone unturned when it comes to their finances, carefully analyzing financial data, budgeting meticulously, and tracking their expenses. This attention to detail allows them to make better financial management decisions, identify areas for improvement, and stay on top of their financial goals.

Type 1 individuals possess a deep-seated drive to achieve their goals, which is advantageous for financial success. They set clear financial objectives and diligently work towards them, staying focused on long-term financial planning. This goal-orientation propels them forward, motivating them to make necessary sacrifices and stay committed to their financial path.

Thoroughness and accuracy are qualities that Type 1 individuals bring to all aspects of their lives. In the financial realm, this trait serves them well. They apply their commitment to being thorough and accurate to financial tasks such as tax planning, portfolio management, and investment analysis. By leaving no stone unturned and ensuring accuracy in their financial endeavors, they increase their chances of favorable outcomes and financial success.

Type 1 individuals have a remarkable level of self-discipline. They possess the ability to delay gratification, resist impulsive spending, and adhere to their financial plans. This self-discipline is crucial in achieving financial goals, as it allows them to stay on track and make consistent progress. By creating and sticking to a budget, adopting smart savings habits, and avoiding impulsive spending, Type 1 individuals cultivate the self-discipline necessary for financial success.

Integrity and ethical behavior are deeply ingrained in Type 1 individuals. They approach their financial lives with a sense of honesty, transparency, and responsibility. This quality enables them to build trust with others, attract ethical business opportunities, and make responsible financial choices. By aligning their financial decisions with their values, Type 1 individuals cultivate a sense of integrity that contributes to their overall financial success.

Type 1 individuals are committed to personal growth and self-improvement. This commitment translates into the financial realm, where they continuously seek knowledge, stay updated on market trends, and adapt their financial strategies accordingly. Their commitment to continuous improvement allows them to stay ahead of the curve and make informed financial decisions.

Balancing their perfectionistic tendencies with flexibility is a challenge that Type 1 individuals must confront. While perfectionism can be a strength, it can also inhibit financial success if taken to an extreme. Type 1 individuals must learn to balance their pursuit of excellence with flexibility, adaptability, and resilience in the face of financial changes or setbacks. By embracing flexibility, they can adjust their strategies when needed and make the necessary financial adjustments to maintain stability and progress towards their goals.

For Type 1 individuals, cultivating self-compassion is vital. The high standards they set for themselves can often lead to feelings of self-criticism or judgment when it comes to their financial life. However, practicing self-compassion and accepting that financial imperfections are a natural part of life can help alleviate these feelings and promote a healthier relationship with money.

Finding a balance between responsible budgeting and allowing themselves to enjoy their money is another challenge Type 1 individuals often face. They may be inclined to restrict their spending and deny themselves pleasures in order to maintain financial security and adhere to their perfectionistic tendencies. However, it is vital for Type 1 individuals to recognize the importance of enjoying the fruits of their labor and allowing themselves to indulge in experiences that bring them joy and fulfillment. This balance between responsible budgeting and enjoying their money is essential for maintaining long-term financial well-being and overall life satisfaction.

Investment decisions can also pose a challenge to Type 1 individuals. Their fear of making mistakes or not finding the perfect investment opportunity can lead to hesitation and missed opportunities for growth. Type 1 individuals must overcome their perfectionistic tendencies when it comes to investments and learn to accept that some level of risk is inherent in the investment process. Seeking professional advice and guidance from trusted financial advisors can help Type 1 individuals navigate this challenge and make informed investment decisions that align with their long-term financial goals.

Flexibility is another crucial aspect that Type 1 individuals need to embrace in order to overcome their financial challenges. Life is unpredictable, and unexpected circumstances can disrupt even the most carefully crafted financial plans. Type 1 individuals must learn to adjust their plans and strategies when needed, rather than rigidly holding onto a predefined path. Embracing flexibility allows them to adapt to changing circumstances and make the necessary financial adjustments to maintain stability and progress towards their goals.

In order to overcome these challenges, Type 1 individuals might benefit from seeking professional financial guidance. By collaborating with a trusted financial advisor who understands their personality traits, values, and goals, Type 1 individuals can receive objective insights and strategies to effectively manage their finances. The guidance of a professional can alleviate some of the burden of decision-making and provide the support needed to navigate their perfectionistic tendencies and achieve financial success.

Ultimately, Type 1 individuals must embrace the idea of imperfection in their financial lives. Accepting that mistakes and setbacks are inevitable allows them to let go of the need for perfection and find contentment in their financial outcomes. By cultivating self-awareness, practicing self-compassion, and setting realistic goals, Type 1 individuals can overcome their perfectionistic tendencies and pave the way for personal growth and financial empowerment. Letting go of the fear of failure and embracing the lessons that can be learned from mistakes, Type 1 individuals can transform their relationship with money and find fulfillment in the journey of building wealth.

Harnessing the strengths of Type 1 for financial success requires embracing the positive qualities of responsibility, prudence, attention to detail, goal-orientation, thoroughness, self-discipline, integrity, commitment to continuous improvement, and flexibility. By understanding and utilizing these strengths, Type 1 individuals can navigate financial challenges, achieve their financial goals, and ultimately find true financial empowerment and a sense of fulfillment in their monetary journey.

Practical Tips for Type 1's Financial Growth

1. Understand your financial mindset: Take time to reflect on how your perfectionism might impact your financial decision-making. Recognize any tendencies towards rigidity or excessive self-criticism, and work on cultivating a more balanced and self-compassionate approach to money.

2. Set SMART financial goals: When setting financial goals, make sure they are Specific, Measurable, Achievable, Relevant, and Time-bound. Consider your personal values and aspirations to ensure your goals align with what truly matters to you.

3. Create a comprehensive budget: Develop a step-by-step process for creating a budget that promotes organization and financial discipline. Track your expenses meticulously and ensure a balanced approach to spending, allowing for both responsible saving and the occasional indulgence.

4. Make financial decisions aligned with your values: Utilize your thoroughness and attention to detail to research and analyze financial options, but be mindful of using this as an excuse for analysis paralysis. Find a balance between thorough

research and taking action, making decisions that align with your values and long-term financial goals.

5. Invest in a way that suits your risk tolerance: Consider investment options that offer security and stability, as these may resonate with your preference for predictability. Develop an investment strategy that aligns with your risk tolerance and long-term financial goals, seeking guidance from trusted financial advisors if needed.

6. Manage and pay off debt responsibly: Develop a debt repayment plan that takes into account your financial obligations, negotiate with creditors when possible, and prioritize debt reduction. Maintain a healthy perspective on mistakes and imperfections, recognizing that financial setbacks are opportunities for growth and learning.

7. Cultivate a healthy mindset towards money: Practice self-compassion, embracing a growth mindset that allows for mistakes and imperfections. Seek support from professionals or therapists to address any perfectionism or anxiety related to finances, and surround yourself with a supportive network of individuals who understand and appreciate your financial aspirations and challenges.

8. Incorporate philanthropy and giving back: Integrate philanthropy into your financial plans and strategies, finding causes and organizations that resonate with your values and interests. Giving back can not only make a positive impact on the world but can also bring a sense of fulfillment and purpose to your financial journey.

9. Learn from mistakes and adjust strategies: Embrace mistakes as opportunities for growth and learning. Adjust your strategies and make necessary changes to achieve financial growth and balance, recognizing that the path to financial success is not linear but requires adaptability and resilience.

10. Build a support network: Surround yourself with individuals who understand and appreciate your financial goals and challenges. Consider joining financial communities or seeking accountability partners to provide ongoing encouragement and guidance.

11. Celebrate your financial successes: Acknowledge your hard work and commitment by celebrating your financial successes, both big and small. Find joy and gratitude in achieving financial milestones and fulfilling your financial aspirations, allowing yourself to enjoy the fruits of your labor.

12. Continue the journey of financial growth: Remember that financial growth is an ongoing journey that extends beyond the practical tips provided. Stay curious, continue learning and adapting to changes in the financial landscape, and regularly revisit and revise your strategies to ensure continued financial well-being and fulfillment.

13. Learn from case studies and real-life examples: Seek out case studies and real-life examples of Type 1 individuals who have implemented practical tips and achieved financial growth. These examples can provide inspiration and illustrate how the strategies can be applied in different financial situations.

14. Explore further resources: Expand your knowledge and understanding of financial growth and personal development by exploring additional resources, books, and websites recommended for Type 1 individuals. Continued self-discovery and learning will enhance your financial journey beyond the book.

Type 1 individuals have unique strengths and challenges when it comes to their financial growth. By embracing their perfectionistic tendencies and balancing them with flexibility, self-compassion, and a growth mindset, Type 1 individuals can cultivate a healthy and empowered relationship with money. The practical tips outlined in this chapter provide a roadmap for Type 1 individuals to achieve financial success while staying true to their values and aspirations. Embrace the journey, celebrate your successes, and continue learning and adapting to create a sustainable and fulfilling financial future.

Chapter 3: The Helper (Type 2)

The Helper's Money Mindset

As they delve deeper into the Enneagram and its relationship with money, they now turn our attention to Type 2 individuals, commonly known as "The Helper." These individuals are characterized by their strong desire to be helpful and supportive of others, making them natural caregivers and nurturers. In their pursuit of assisting others, Type 2s often neglect their own needs, including their financial well-being.

The financial mindset of Type 2 individuals is deeply rooted in their innate desire to be of service. Their selfless nature often leads them to prioritize the needs of others over their own financial stability. It is not uncommon for a Type 2 to willingly sacrifice their own financial success or security if it means being able to support someone else.

Underlying Type 2's relationship with money are certain beliefs that shape their financial decisions. For many Type 2s, financial success is not viewed as being as important as being there for others. They may believe that true fulfillment comes from giving, rather than amassing wealth or material possessions. These beliefs can influence their financial choices, often leading them to prioritize the needs of others over their own.

The motivations that drive Type 2 individuals in their financial decisions stem from their deep desire to be valued and appreciated by others. They find fulfillment in being seen as indispensable and indispensable to those around them. Consequently, this desire can push them to make financial choices that prioritize the needs of others over their own, ensuring that they are always available to give and support.

Yet, this selfless nature can pose challenges for Type 2 individuals when it comes to achieving financial balance. The very act of setting boundaries around money can feel uncomfortable and counterintuitive to them. Their focus on helping others can make it difficult for them to prioritize their own financial well-being, leading to financial imbalances and even potential hardships.

To cultivate a healthy and balanced money mindset, Type 2 individuals must find ways to take care of themselves financially while still being able to help others. It is crucial for them to acknowledge that self-care is not selfish, but rather an essential aspect of their overall well-being. Practical strategies can include setting financial boundaries, creating a budget that includes their own needs, and seeking professional advice to ensure their financial stability.

When Type 2 individuals prioritize their own financial well-being, they actually empower themselves to help others in a more sustainable and impactful way. By taking care of their own needs, they can build a solid foundation from which they can extend their support and assistance to those in need. This self-care enhances their ability to make a meaningful and lasting difference in the lives of others.

As Type 2 individuals grow and evolve in their relationship with money, they can experience a profound transformation. They begin to value their own financial needs and make decisions that align with their long-term goals. They realize that by ensuring their own financial stability, they are better equipped to support others and create lasting change in the world.

By aligning their financial decisions with their core values of helping and supporting others, Type 2 individuals can find true fulfillment in their financial journey. They discover a synergy between their desire to be of service and their financial goals. Money becomes a tool that empowers them to make a positive impact on the world, enabling them to contribute to creating a more caring and equitable society.

It is important for Type 2 individuals to strike a balance between their selfless nature and self-care. While their instinct to help others is admirable, they must also prioritize their own financial well-being. By finding this equilibrium, they can continue to live with compassion and generosity, while also ensuring their own stability and security.

Navigating the financial journey as a Type 2 individual may have its challenges, but it is crucial to remain committed to your financial well-being. Remember that taking care of yourself financially does not diminish your ability to assist others; it only makes you better equipped to make a lasting impact. Stay focused, seek support when needed, and know that your financial journey holds the potential for immense personal growth and positive change in the world.

Financial Struggles of Type 2

Type 2 individuals, often known as "The Helper," possess an innate desire to care for and support others. This generous and compassionate nature is a beautiful attribute, but it can also create financial challenges for Type 2s. In this chapter, they will delve into the specific financial struggles that Type 2 individuals commonly face, shedding light on their patterns and tendencies, and empowering them to find balance and self-worth in their financial journey.

One of the biggest challenges for Type 2s is what I like to call the "Generosity Trap." Their natural inclination to help and support others can often lead them to neglect their own financial well-being. They prioritize the needs and desires of others above their own, which can result in financial imbalances and potential hardships. Type 2s must recognize that it is not selfish to prioritize their own financial needs; in fact, it is essential for their overall well-being and their ability to make a sustainable impact on the lives of others.

Putting others' needs before their own is another struggle that Type 2 individuals commonly face. They have a tendency to prioritize the financial needs of others, whether it be family, friends, or charitable causes, over their own. This can lead to financial insecurity and dependency, as they neglect their own financial goals and responsibilities. Type 2s must learn to strike a balance between helping others and taking care of their own financial well-being. It is important for them to set boundaries and allocate resources for their own needs and future financial stability.

Difficulty setting boundaries is a significant challenge for Type 2s when it comes to their finances. They may feel guilty saying no to others' financial requests or feel obligated to financially support others, even if it stretches them beyond their means. This can lead to overextending their financial resources, taking on loans or debt, and sacrificing their own financial security. Type 2s must develop assertiveness skills and learn to communicate their boundaries and limitations effectively. It is crucial for them to realize that saying no to others' financial demands does not make them any less compassionate or caring.

Overextending financial resources is a common pitfall for Type 2 individuals. Their generous nature may drive them to provide financial help beyond their means or take on financial burdens for others. This can lead to a cycle of financial strain and difficulty managing their own financial well-being. Type 2s must develop a realistic understanding of their financial capacity and be mindful of their own financial goals and limitations. It is essential for them to seek professional advice and guidance to ensure that they are making informed financial decisions that align with their own long-term stability.

Type 2s often underestimate their personal value, which can contribute to their financial struggles. They may undervalue their skills and abilities, settling for lower-paying jobs or underpricing their services. This lack of self-worth can hinder their financial growth and limit their earning potential. Type 2 individuals must recognize their inherent value and worth, both in their personal relationships and in the marketplace. They deserve to be compensated fairly for their contributions and should strive to find a balance between helping others and valuing their own financial well-being.

Neglecting self-care, including financial self-care, is another challenge that Type 2 individuals face. Their focus on others can lead them to prioritize the needs of others over their own, neglecting their financial responsibilities and goals. Type 2s must recognize the importance of taking care of themselves financially, just as they take care of others. This means saving and investing for the future, creating a budget that includes their own needs and desires, and seeking professional guidance to ensure their financial stability.

Another struggle for Type 2 individuals is a fear of financial independence. Their need to be needed and connected to others can make it challenging for them to assert financial independence. They may rely on others for financial support or feel uncomfortable taking control of their own financial decisions. Type 2s must confront this fear and recognize that financial independence does not diminish their ability to care for and support others. In fact, it empowers them to create a solid foundation from which they can extend their generosity and make a meaningful impact on the world.

Guilt surrounding financial success is a common emotional burden for Type 2s. They may feel guilty when they achieve financial success, as if it is taking away from others or betraying their caretaker role. This guilt can hinder their ability to grow and thrive financially, as they may hold themselves back out of a sense of obligation. Type 2s must release this guilt and understand that their financial success does not diminish their compassion or their ability to help others. In fact, it expands their capacity to make a positive impact in the world.

Finding balance and self-worth is the ultimate goal for Type 2 individuals when it comes to their finances. They must learn to prioritize their own financial well-being while still embracing their innate desire to help and support others. It is essential for Type 2s to develop a healthy sense of self-worth that encompasses both their financial goals and their compassionate nature. This can be achieved through strategies such as setting boundaries, seeking support from like-minded individuals, and seeking professional help when needed. By finding this balance, Type 2 individuals can break free from their financial struggles and create a healthier and more fulfilling relationship with money.

Navigating the specific financial struggles of Type 2s requires practical tips and tools. In the next chapter, I will provide guidance on budgeting, seeking professional help, and developing assertiveness skills. These strategies will empower Type 2 individuals to navigate their financial challenges and find a sense of financial well-being that aligns with their core values of helping and supporting others.

It is important for Type 2s to remember that their strengths as empathetic and compassionate individuals can be leveraged in their financial journey. In the following chapter, I will explore how Type 2s can use their unique attributes to overcome their financial struggles and create a healthier money mindset. By embracing their strengths, Type 2 individuals can transform their financial journey and make a positive impact in the world.

Support and community are vital for Type 2 individuals as they navigate their specific financial struggles. Connecting with others who understand and share similar challenges can provide guidance, encouragement, and a sense of belonging. Type 2s should seek out resources and communities that can support their financial growth and provide tools and insights specific to their needs. By surrounding themselves with like-minded individuals, they can strengthen their financial journey and find solace in knowing that they are not alone.

Breaking the cycle of financial struggles is possible for Type 2 individuals. By recognizing their patterns, implementing positive changes, and embracing a new mindset around money, they can break free from the limitations that have held them back. It requires commitment, self-reflection, and a willingness to redefine their relationship with money. Type 2s have the power to create a brighter financial future for themselves and make a lasting impact on the world through their generosity and compassion.

I encourage you to reflect on your own financial behaviors and patterns. Take the time to explore your own tendencies and challenges when it comes to money. By gaining a deeper understanding of yourself, you can begin to take steps towards financial empowerment and find a sense of balance and self-worth in your financial journey.

Leveraging Type 2's Strengths for Financial well-being

Type 2 individuals possess unique strengths and qualities that can contribute to their financial success. These individuals are empathetic, compassionate, and nurturing, making them highly attuned to the needs and emotions of others. In the realm of finance, these qualities can be leveraged to build strong relationships with clients, customers, and colleagues, ultimately leading to greater financial opportunities. However, Type 2s must also be mindful of the challenges they may face, such as overextending their resources or neglecting their own financial well-being. By understanding and embracing their strengths, Type 2 individuals can navigate their financial journey with confidence and create a positive impact in the world.

One of the key strengths of Type 2 individuals is their deep capacity for empathy. They have a unique ability to understand and connect with others on an emotional level. In the context of finance, this empathetic nature can be a valuable asset. By genuinely understanding the needs and desires of their clients, Type 2s can establish strong relationships built on trust and authenticity. This, in turn, fosters customer loyalty and can lead to repeat business and referrals. Type 2s excel in industries that require high levels of client interaction, such as sales, customer service, and coaching. Whether it's providing financial advice, negotiating deals, or offering support during tough times, their empathy allows them to connect with others on a deeper level, leading to financial gain and personal fulfillment.

Type 2 individuals possess a natural talent for building connections and nurturing relationships. This ability to network effectively can be a powerful tool in the realm of finance. By leveraging their social skills and genuine interest in others, Type 2s can expand their professional network, opening doors to new business opportunities and financial growth. They excel in roles that require collaboration and relationship-building, such as client management, marketing, and entrepreneurship. Type 2s should actively seek out networking opportunities, attend industry events, and connect with like-minded professionals. By harnessing their connection-building skills, they can create a strong support system and unlock doors to financial success.

Type 2 individuals possess a heightened emotional intelligence, allowing them to navigate complex emotional landscapes with ease. In the realm of finance, emotional intelligence can be a powerful tool. Type 2s have the ability to read non-verbal cues, understand others' perspectives, and make informed decisions based on emotional data. Whether it's negotiating deals, managing investments, or developing financial plans, their emotional intelligence gives them a competitive edge. Type 2s should trust their intuition and emotional insights when making financial decisions, as they often have a deep understanding of the underlying motivations and emotional needs that drive such choices. They can further enhance their emotional intelligence by actively seeking feedback and self-reflection, allowing them to make sound financial choices that align with their values and priorities.

Generosity and giving are at the core of Type 2 individuals. They have an innate desire to help and support others, leading them to engage in acts of kindness and selflessness. In the realm of finance, this natural inclination towards generosity can lead to significant financial success. By giving back to their communities, whether through charitable donations, pro bono services, or volunteer work, Type 2s create positive financial opportunities. Their act of giving often attracts like-minded individuals and organizations who align with their values, thereby opening doors to collaborative ventures, strategic partnerships, and increased financial abundance. Type 2s should embrace their generous nature and seek out opportunities to make a positive impact in the world, knowing that their acts of kindness can pave the way for financial success.

While Type 2 individuals excel in their ability to care for and support others, they may face challenges when it comes to prioritizing their own financial well-being. Their selfless nature can lead them to overextend their resources, take on loans or debt, and sacrifice their own financial security. To overcome this challenge, Type 2s must develop assertiveness skills and learn to communicate their boundaries and limitations effectively. It is crucial for them to realize that saying no to others' financial demands does not make them any less compassionate or caring. Establishing healthy boundaries and prioritizing their own financial needs is essential for Type 2 individuals to achieve true financial well-being.

Another strength of Type 2 individuals is their ability to collaborate and work well in teams. They thrive in situations where they can support and empower others towards a common goal. In the realm of finance, building successful partnerships can lead to financial growth and mutual benefit. Type 2s should seek out collaborative opportunities, whether it's working with like-minded professionals, forming strategic alliances, or joining forces with complementary businesses. By leveraging their collaborative skills, they can tap into a wider pool of resources, knowledge, and connections, ultimately leading to financial success for all involved.

Type 2 individuals possess a natural intuition and insight that can guide them in their financial decision-making. They often have a strong gut feeling about what is right or wrong, and this can be a valuable asset. Type 2s should trust their instincts when it comes to identifying profitable opportunities, making wise investments, and navigating financial challenges. Honing and trusting their intuition requires self-awareness and practice. Type 2s should take the time to reflect, meditate, and tune in to their inner voice. By embracing their intuitive nature, Type 2 individuals can make confident and informed financial decisions that align with their core values and lead to greater financial success.

Type 2 individuals have a unique capacity for empowering others and supporting their financial goals. Their empathetic and nurturing nature allows them to coach, mentor, or provide financial guidance to those in need. By leveraging this innate ability, Type 2s can not only make a positive impact on the lives of others but also create financial success for themselves. Whether it's through financial coaching, mentorship programs, or educational initiatives, Type 2s can leverage their abilities to help others achieve their financial dreams and aspirations. Through these acts of empowerment, Type 2 individuals can create a ripple effect of financial well-being and abundance that extends far beyond their own lives.

For Type 2 individuals, cultivating a strong sense of self-worth is crucial in attracting financial abundance. They may often undervalue their skills and abilities, either settling for lower-paying jobs or underpricing their services. This lack of self-worth can hinder their financial growth and limit their earning potential. Type 2s must recognize their inherent value and worth, both in their personal relationships and in the marketplace. They deserve to be compensated fairly for their contributions and should strive to find a balance between helping others and valuing their own financial well-being. By cultivating a mindset of self-worth and abundance, Type 2 individuals can attract greater financial opportunities and create a healthier relationship with money.

Type 2 individuals may struggle with finding a balance between financial independence and their desire for connection. As natural caretakers, they may rely on others for financial support or feel uncomfortable taking control of their own financial decisions. However, it is crucial for Type 2s to confront this fear and recognize that financial independence does not diminish their ability to care for and support others. In fact, it empowers them to create a solid foundation from which they can extend their generosity and make a meaningful impact on the world. Type 2s should prioritize their financial well-being and actively seek opportunities to enhance their financial independence while maintaining connection with others. By setting healthy boundaries and defining financial independence in alignment with their strengths and values, Type 2 individuals can achieve a sense of financial freedom that allows them to blossom both personally and professionally.

Type 2 individuals possess a unique set of strengths and qualities that can be leveraged for financial well-being. Empathy, networking, emotional intelligence, generosity, collaboration, intuition, empowerment, self-worth, and maintaining balance are all key aspects of their financial journey. By embracing these strengths and adopting a proactive mindset, Type 2s can navigate their financial struggles with confidence, resilience, and compassion. As they gain a deeper understanding of their own financial behaviors and patterns, they can make conscious choices that lead to a healthier and more fulfilling relationship with money. It is through this journey of self-discovery and empowerment that Type 2 individuals can break free from financial limitations and create a brighter financial future, while still making a meaningful impact on the world through their inherent capacity to care, support, and empower others.

Practical Steps for Type 2's Financial Empowerment

To achieve financial empowerment, Type 2 individuals must take practical steps that align with their unique strengths and challenges. These steps will help them overcome their tendencies to prioritize others' needs over their own and establish healthy financial boundaries. Here are some practical steps that Type 2s can take to achieve financial empowerment:

Step 1: Self-awareness and reflection

The first step towards financial empowerment for Type 2 individuals is to develop self-awareness and reflect on their financial patterns and behaviors. They can start by asking themselves questions like: What are my financial goals? How do I make financial decisions? Do I put others' financial needs before my own? By gaining a deeper understanding of their financial attitudes and habits, Type 2s can identify areas where they may need to make changes and set the foundation for their financial journey.

Step 2: Setting financial goals aligned with core values

Type 2s should set financial goals that align with their core values and aspirations. They can start by identifying their priorities and what they truly want to achieve financially. Setting clear and specific goals, such as saving for a down payment on a house or starting a business, can help Type 2s stay focused and motivated on their journey to financial empowerment.

Step 3: Creating a budget

Creating a budget is an important step for Type 2 individuals to gain control over their financial situation. They should track their income and expenses, identify areas where they can cut back on spending, and allocate funds towards their financial goals. Type 2s should also ensure that they include an allowance for their generosity and giving nature, but also establish limits to prevent overextension.

Step 4: Building financial independence

Type 2s should focus on building their financial independence by taking active steps to increase their income and save for the future. They can explore opportunities to advance in their careers or start their own businesses. By prioritizing their own financial growth, Type 2s can build a solid foundation that allows them to continue to support and empower others.

Step 5: Saying 'no' to financial requests

One of the challenges Type 2 individuals face is saying 'no' to financial requests from others. To achieve financial empowerment, they need to set healthy boundaries and feel comfortable speaking up when it comes to their own financial well-being. Type 2s should learn to kindly decline requests that do not align with their financial goals or that overextend their resources. By doing so, they can protect their financial stability and create a healthier relationship with money.

Step 6: Seeking professional financial advice

Type 2s can benefit from seeking professional financial advice to help them navigate their financial journey. They should look for a financial advisor or planner who understands their unique strengths and challenges and can provide guidance tailored to their needs. By collaborating with a financial professional, Type 2s can gain valuable insights and knowledge to make informed financial decisions.

Step 7: Practicing self-care and maintaining balance

Type 2 individuals often prioritize the needs of others over their own, which can lead to neglecting their own self-care and well-being. To achieve financial empowerment, Type 2s must prioritize self-care and establish a healthy balance between caring for others and caring for themselves. They should set aside time for rest, relaxation, and activities that bring joy and rejuvenation. By taking care of themselves, Type 2s can maintain their own financial stability and continue to support others from a place of abundance.

Step 8: Celebrating milestones and achievements

Type 2 individuals should celebrate their financial milestones and achievements along their journey. By acknowledging and appreciating their progress, they reinforce positive financial habits and motivate themselves to continue on their path to empowerment. Type 2s can celebrate in meaningful ways, such as treating themselves to a small indulgence or sharing their success with loved ones.

Step 9: Continuing to learn and grow

Type 2s should continue to learn and grow in their financial knowledge and skills. They can engage in self-education by reading books, taking courses, and exploring resources that enhance their financial literacy. By continually expanding their financial knowledge, Type 2s can make more informed decisions and adapt to changing financial landscapes.

Step 10: Building a supportive financial network

Type 2 individuals can also benefit from building a supportive network of individuals who can provide guidance and accountability in their financial journey. They can seek out like-minded individuals or join financial support groups where they can share experiences, learn from others, and receive encouragement. By surrounding themselves with a supportive financial network, Type 2s can gain inspiration and motivation to continue on their path towards empowerment.

Type 2 individuals have unique strengths and challenges when it comes to their financial journey. By taking practical steps that align with their core values and prioritizing their own financial well-being, Type 2s can achieve financial empowerment. Through self-awareness, setting goals, creating a budget, building financial independence, saying 'no' when necessary, seeking professional advice, practicing self-care, celebrating achievements, and continuing to learn and grow, Type 2s can break free from financial limitations and create a brighter financial future while still making a meaningful impact on the world through their inherent capacity to care for and empower others.

Chapter 4: The Achiever (Type 3)

The Achiever's Money Mentality

At the core of a Type 3's financial decisions lie two powerful drivers: the need to be seen as successful and the fear of failure. These drivers stem from a deep yearning for validation and external recognition. Type 3s are acutely aware of the importance society places on material wealth and the positive perception it can bring. They are driven to amass monetary success not only for the financial comforts it may provide but also as a symbol of their personal worth.

Societal expectations play a significant role in shaping the financial mindset of Type 3 individuals. The Achiever's desire to keep up appearances and meet cultural norms can lead them to make financial choices based on external perception rather than internal fulfillment. They may find themselves trapped in an eternal cycle of seeking validation through financial achievements, often sacrificing their own authenticity in the process.

The fear of financial failure looms large in the minds of Type 3s. This fear compels them to work tirelessly, constantly striving to prove their worth through monetary success. They are driven by a deep-seated need for affirmation and validation, which they seek to achieve through their financial achievements. This fear can consume them, fueling their relentless pursuit of financial success.

Competition plays a significant role in shaping a Type 3's financial mindset. They thrive on outperforming others and being recognized as the best. This competitive nature can drive them to make bold financial choices, aiming to surpass their peers and secure their position at the top. While competition can be a powerful motivator, it is essential for Type 3s to reflect on whether their financial decisions are driven purely by a desire to win or if they genuinely align with their personal values.

Balancing authenticity and financial success becomes a delicate dance for Type 3 individuals. It is crucial for them to pause and reflect on their desires and motivations. Strategies that can aid Type 3s in this navigation include aligning their financial goals with their personal values, practicing self-reflection, and seeking support from professionals or engaging in personal development practices. By doing so, they can reconcile their need for financial success with their desire for authentic self-expression.

Overcoming the fear of financial failure is a significant hurdle for Type 3 individuals. To address this fear, they can start by embracing self-acceptance and resilience. Letting go of the need for constant affirmation and reevaluating their definition of success are critical steps on this journey. By adopting a mindset that prioritizes personal growth and fulfillment above external validation, Type 3s can find peace in their financial journey.

Cultivating a healthy relationship with money is essential for Type 3s. Developing a balanced approach to finance involves setting realistic expectations, finding fulfillment beyond financial achievements, and recognizing that wealth does not define personal worth. By embracing these principles, Type 3s can redefine their money mentality and achieve a more harmonious relationship with their financial decisions.

Type 3 individuals possess unique strengths that can contribute to their financial success. Their drive, ambition, and ability to excel can propel them forward in their pursuit of financial goals. However, harnessing these strengths effectively requires self-awareness and personal growth. By staying attuned to their core drivers and cultivating self-reflection practices, Type 3s can enhance their financial decision-making and leverage their inherent abilities for long-term success.

Self-reflection and introspection are indispensable tools for Type 3 individuals on their financial journey. By delving into their motivations, fears, and desires, they gain a deeper understanding of themselves and their relationship with money. Engaging in personal development practices and seeking support from professionals can further enhance the benefits of self-reflection, empowering Type 3s to make conscious and informed financial choices.

To illustrate the intricacies of Type 3's financial choices, case studies and real-life examples can serve as powerful learning tools. By examining the outcomes and lessons of these examples, readers can gain a deeper insight into the mindset and decision-making processes of Type 3 individuals. These case studies provide valuable context and offer opportunities for self-reflection and growth.

Understanding the achiever's money mentality is a crucial step in unraveling the intricacies of their financial decisions. Type 3 individuals' innate drive for success and recognition, coupled with societal expectations, fear of failure, and a competitive spirit, shape their approach to money. By fostering authenticity, overcoming fear, and finding a balance between financial success and personal fulfillment, Type 3s can transform their money mentality into a force that aligns with their values and brings them genuine satisfaction.

Financial Hurdles for Type 3

Balancing authenticity and financial success becomes a delicate dance for Type 3 individuals. It is crucial for us to pause and reflect on our desires and motivations. Are they chasing financial achievements at the expense of our own happiness and well-being? Are they prioritizing appearances over financial stability? These are questions that we must ask ourselves in order to find true fulfillment.

One of the challenges they face is managing multiple projects and financial goals simultaneously. Our ambitious nature often leads us to take on more than they can handle, spreading ourselves thin and neglecting the necessary attention our finances require. This can result in missed opportunities or poor financial planning, ultimately hindering our progress.

Another challenge they encounter is the difficulty in balancing work and personal life. Our relentless drive for success can consume us, causing us to neglect our financial matters. It is easy to get caught up in the pursuit of wealth and recognition, allowing our personal lives to suffer as a result.

Fear of failure is a significant hurdle for many Type 3 individuals when it comes to financial decision-making. They often feel the pressure to maintain a certain financial image, comparing themselves to others and striving to keep up with the lifestyles of those they perceive as successful. This fear can lead us to make impulsive and irrational financial choices, ultimately hindering our long-term financial stability.

Additionally, our desire for recognition can tempt us to overspend on status symbols. they may feel the need to portray an image of success, leading us to splurge on luxury items or experiences that are beyond our means. This behavior can result in financial strain and debt, further perpetuating our fear of failure.

Setting realistic financial goals and sticking to them can be a challenge for Type 3 individuals. Our ambitious nature often leads us to set lofty, sometimes unattainable goals, which can lead to disappointment and frustration. It is important for us to be mindful of our capabilities and create a plan that is both realistic and sustainable.

Amidst all the financial hurdles, it is vital for Type 3 individuals to find fulfillment and satisfaction beyond material achievements. They must learn to value ourselves not only for our outward success but also for our inherent worth as individuals. Building meaningful relationships, pursuing hobbies and passions, and finding purpose outside of our careers can all contribute to a more fulfilling life.

To overcome these financial hurdles, Type 3 individuals must prioritize authenticity and align their financial decisions with their personal values. By gaining a deeper understanding of ourselves and our relationship with money, they can make conscious and informed choices that bring us genuine satisfaction. Seeking support from professionals or engaging in personal development practices can also aid us in navigating our financial journey.

Understanding the financial hurdles faced by Type 3 individuals is crucial for creating a balanced and fulfilling financial life. By recognizing and addressing our drive for success, fear of failure, and desire for recognition, they can transform our money mentality into a force that aligns with our values and brings us true fulfillment.

Capitalizing on Type 3's Strengths for Financial Success

In addition to ambition, Type 3 individuals possess natural charisma and persuasive abilities. These skills can be invaluable in sales, marketing, and entrepreneurial ventures. By leveraging their natural magnetism, they can excel in these areas and generate financial opportunities for themselves. It is important for us to constantly refine their persuasive techniques and develop strategies for maximizing their income potential.

Another strength of Type 3 individuals is their adaptability and versatility. In today's rapidly changing business landscape, being open to new opportunities and constantly evolving is essential for financial success. they must be willing to explore new industries, adapt to changing trends, and embrace innovation. By doing so, they can stay ahead in the competitive market and capitalize on emerging financial opportunities.

Type 3 individuals also possess a strong work ethic, which can be channeled towards building a strong financial foundation. Their disciplined work habits and dedication to achieving our goals can contribute to their financial stability. By maximizing their productivity and finding ways to work smartly, they can create a solid financial base for themselves.

Another strength of Type 3 individuals lies in their ability to network and build valuable connections in the business world. Building a strong professional network is crucial for financial success, as it can bring opportunities for collaboration, partnerships, and career growth. By actively fostering relationships and leveraging our network, they can open doors to financial opportunities that may not have been otherwise available to them.

Type 3 individuals also possess natural leadership skills, which can be used to take on high-level roles that come with financial rewards. By developing and showcasing our leadership abilities, they can advance in our career and increase our earning potential. This may involve seeking leadership roles within our organizations or even starting their own businesses.

Additionally, Type 3 individuals are inherently competitive, and this can be channeled towards financial success. By embracing healthy competition and using it as motivation, they can push themselves to achieve greater financial heights. However, it is important to maintain a balance and avoid unhealthy comparisons or excessive competition that may lead to burnout.

Prioritization and focus are also strengths of Type 3 individuals. By setting clear financial goals, managing their time effectively, and staying focused on our path to financial success, they can make significant strides in achieving our objectives. It is important for them to resist distractions and stay committed to their financial journey.

Furthermore, Type 3 individuals have a natural ability to learn and adapt to new skills and knowledge. In a rapidly changing world, continuous learning and personal development are essential for staying relevant and seizing financial opportunities. By investing in their own growth and acquiring new skills, they can position themselves for financial success.

Last, as Type 3 individuals, the importance of self-awareness and authenticity cannot be overlooked in their pursuit of financial success. It is crucial for them to embrace their true values and passions, as they can lead themselves to greater fulfillment and financial well-being. By aligning their financial decisions with their personal values, they can make conscious and informed choices that bring them genuine satisfaction.

To capitalize on these strengths and achieve financial success, Type 3 individuals must be proactive and strategic in their approach. It is important for them to set realistic goals, create actionable plans, and seek support from professionals or engage in personal development practices when needed. By utilizing their strengths and aligning their financial decisions with their personal values, they can create a balanced and fulfilling financial life.

Actionable Strategies for Type 3's Financial Growth

1. Embrace networking and building relationships: Type 3 individuals should actively seek out opportunities to connect with others in the financial industry. By attending conferences, joining professional organizations, and engaging in networking events, Type 3s can cultivate relationships that can lead to new financial opportunities. It is important for Type 3s to approach networking with authenticity and a genuine interest in building meaningful connections.

2. Develop leadership skills: Type 3 individuals should aim to take on leadership roles in their careers or within their own businesses. By showcasing their natural leadership abilities, Type 3s can position themselves for promotions, higher salaries, and increased earning potential. It is important for Type 3s to continuously develop their leadership skills through courses, workshops, or mentorship programs.

3. Embrace healthy competition: Type 3s can use their competitive nature as motivation for financial success. By

setting goals, tracking progress, and comparing themselves with their own performance rather than others, Type 3s can push themselves to achieve greater financial heights. However, it is crucial for Type 3s to maintain a healthy balance and avoid excessive competition that may lead to burnout or an unhealthy focus on material success.

4. Prioritize and stay focused: Type 3 individuals should set clear financial goals and prioritize their actions accordingly. By managing their time effectively, avoiding distractions, and staying committed to their financial journey, Type 3s can make significant strides in achieving their objectives. It is important for Type 3s to resist the temptation of chasing every opportunity and instead focus on the ones that align with their long-term financial goals.

5. Invest in continuous learning and personal development: Type 3 individuals should prioritize their own growth and development in the financial domain. By investing in courses, attending seminars, reading relevant books, and seeking mentorship, Type 3s can acquire new skills and stay up-to-date with the changing landscape of finance. It is important for Type 3s to remain adaptable and open to learning in order to seize financial opportunities.

6. Align financial decisions with personal values: Type 3s should make conscious and informed financial choices that align with their personal values and passions. By staying true to their core beliefs and desires, Type 3s can create a balanced and fulfilling financial life. It is important for Type 3s to regularly

evaluate their financial decisions and ensure they are in line with their personal values and long-term aspirations.

7. Seek professional guidance when needed: Type 3 individuals should not hesitate to seek support from financial professionals when needed. Whether it is consulting with a financial advisor, accountant, or coach, Type 3s can benefit from their expertise and guidance in achieving their financial goals. It is important for Type 3s to recognize that seeking help is a sign of strength and a proactive step towards financial success.

By implementing these actionable strategies, Type 3 individuals can harness their strengths, overcome their fears, and achieve their financial goals. It is crucial for Type 3s to approach their financial growth with a balanced mindset, being mindful of their values and maintaining a sense of authenticity throughout their journey.

Transformative Journeys: Type 3's Pursuit of Financial Authenticity

In this chapter, they have explored the transformative journeys of Type 3 individuals in their pursuit of financial authenticity. The Achievers, as they are known, are driven by a need for success, recognition, and admiration, often seeking external validation in their financial pursuits. However, through their journeys, they have witnessed how some Type 3s have shifted their focus from external measures of success to aligning their financial pursuits with their authentic selves.

One of the key challenges faced by Type 3 individuals is balancing external expectations with their internal values. They often find themselves navigating societal and cultural pressures to achieve financial success, which can sometimes conflict with their true desires and passion. However, through the transformative stories shared in this chapter, they have discovered how some Type 3s have found ways to strike a balance between external expectations and their internal values, allowing them to create a sense of financial authenticity that brings true fulfillment.

Another aspect of the Type 3 journey is overcoming the fear of failure. Type 3 individuals have a deep-rooted fear of failure, which can drive them to relentlessly pursue financial success. However, through the transformative stories in this chapter, they have witnessed how some Type 3s have courageously confronted this fear, allowing them to redefine their definition of success. They have found that true financial fulfillment goes beyond external measures and instead lies in personal growth, purpose, and contribution.

A significant transformation for Type 3 individuals is the embrace of vulnerability and self-acceptance. In their pursuit of financial authenticity, they have learned to let go of the need to constantly present a picture-perfect image. Instead, they have discovered that authenticity brings deeper connections and a profound sense of financial fulfillment. No longer bound by the fear of being seen as imperfect, Type 3s have found the courage to be vulnerable and embrace their true selves.

Key to the transformative journeys of Type 3 individuals is the alignment of financial goals with personal values. They have learned that true financial authenticity lies in pursuing goals that are congruent with their core values and passions. By integrating personal interests and passions into their financial paths, Type 3s have created a sense of alignment and fulfillment that transcends traditional measures of success.

Throughout their transformative journeys, Type 3 individuals have also had to navigate the pressure to conform. They have faced societal expectations and norms that can hinder their pursuit of financial authenticity. However, through the stories shared in this chapter, they have witnessed how Type 3s have found the courage to break free from these constraints. They have embraced their unique journey towards financial fulfillment, paving their own path rather than succumbing to external pressures.

The pursuit of financial authenticity has a profound impact on personal relationships. As Type 3s undergo transformative journeys, their relationships with loved ones, colleagues, and themselves are deeply affected. By aligning financial pursuits with personal values, Type 3s have fostered deeper connections, authenticity, and a sense of purpose in their relationships.

Readers will find valuable lessons and insights from the transformative stories of Type 3 individuals in this chapter. These stories serve as inspiration and guidance for readers who also seek financial fulfillment while staying true to their authentic selves. By implementing the actionable strategies presented in this chapter, Type 3 individuals can harness their strengths, overcome their fears, and achieve their financial goals with a balanced mindset and a sense of authenticity.

In the next chapter, they will delve into the unique financial perspectives and challenges faced by Type 4 individuals, the Individualists, as they embark on their own transformative journeys towards financial authenticity.

Chapter 5: The Individualist (Type 4)

The Individualist's Relationship With Money

Understanding the financial attitudes and decisions of Type 4 individuals is crucial not only for themselves but also for those who interact with them in financial matters. These individuals have a deep emotional and psychological connection to money, and their financial choices are often driven by their need for self-expression and validation. By delving deep into their unique perspectives and motivations, they can gain insights into how to better support and guide Type 4s in their pursuit of financial well-being.

Emotional intensity lies at the core of a Type 4 individualist's relationship with money. Their heightened sensitivity and ability to tap into their emotions allow them to experience the world in a way that others may find foreign. This intensity, combined with their yearning for authenticity and uniqueness, can manifest in their financial choices. For Type 4s, money becomes a vehicle for self-expression and a means to cultivate their personal identity. This can lead them to make decisions that prioritize personal satisfaction and the pursuit of what feels meaningful over more traditional measures of financial success.

Meaning lies at the heart of a Type 4 individualist's financial priorities. They are driven by a deep need to find purpose and significance in their choices and actions, including how they manage their money. Material possessions often pale in comparison to the value they place on experiences and moments that enrich their lives. While others may strive for extravagant displays of wealth, Type 4 individuals challenge convention by embracing a simpler, more meaningful approach to money. They seek to forge a path that aligns with their unique values and aspirations, even if it means veering away from societal expectations.

Type 4 individuals are particularly susceptible to emotional spending, using money as a means to validate their self-worth and seek emotional fulfillment. Their deep connection to their emotions can lead them to use money as a tool to express and regulate their innermost feelings. Seekers of beauty and novelty, they may find themselves succumbing to impulsive purchases in pursuit of fleeting moments of joy or to compensate for their perceived lack of fulfillment. It is essential for Type 4s to become mindful of these tendencies and to develop strategies for channeling their emotional energy in healthier ways.

Financial insecurity often strikes at the core of a Type 4 individualist's sense of self-worth. Feeling different and distinct from others, they may struggle with finding stability and security in their financial lives. The pursuit of their creative passions or unconventional career choices can sometimes lead to periods of financial instability, creating a deep sense of vulnerability and self-doubt. It is crucial to support Type 4s in understanding that their worth extends beyond their financial circumstances and assist them in developing strategies to establish a more secure foundation.

Type 4 individuals possess a natural affinity for creative pursuits. Their ability to tap into their emotions and harness their unique perspective often sets them on a path to explore creative careers or financial endeavors. While this journey can offer immense fulfillment and a genuine expression of their individuality, it also presents certain challenges. The volatile nature of creative industries combined with the individualist's intense emotions can create financial uncertainty. Supporting Type 4s in navigating these challenges requires a delicate balance between encouraging their creative pursuits and helping them establish stability and long-term financial security.

Understanding the financial struggles and tendencies of Type 4 individuals is essential in our exploration of the Enneagram's relationship with money. Type 4s, known as the Individualist, possess unique qualities that shape their approach to finances. With their deep emotional connection, pursuit of authenticity, and desire for meaningful work, Type 4s encounter both challenges and opportunities when it comes to their financial well-being. In this segment, they will delve into the intricacies of their financial struggles and explore ways to navigate them effectively.

Type 4 individuals have a profound emotional connection with money. Their self-expressive nature, coupled with their intense feelings, influences their financial decisions and behaviors. For them, money is not merely a means of survival or accumulation of wealth; it is a way to express their deepest desires and find meaning in their lives. This emotional attachment can result in impulsive spending, as they seek to capture moments of joy or compensate for underlying feelings of emptiness. Understanding and managing these emotional tendencies is crucial for Type 4s to develop a healthy relationship with money.

Type 4 individuals prioritize authenticity in their purchasing decisions. They seek experiences, possessions, and investments that align with their unique values, aspirations, and personal aesthetic. While this pursuit can lead to a rich and fulfilling life, it also comes with potential financial challenges. Type 4s may find themselves overspending in an attempt to create a particular image or to validate their own self-worth. This can result in accumulating debt or living beyond their means. By understanding and balancing their desire for authenticity with practical considerations, Type 4s can achieve financial stability while remaining true to themselves.

Type 4 individuals are often focused on the present moment, prioritizing their immediate emotional needs over practical considerations. Long-term financial planning may seem distant or even irrelevant to them, as they place more value on the freedom to explore their passions and express their unique identity. This can lead to challenges in building financial stability and security. It is important to support Type 4s in developing a balanced approach, recognizing the importance of both embracing their individuality and planning for their future financial well-being.

Type 4 individuals have a deep longing for work that aligns with their personal values and passions. They seek careers that provide a sense of purpose and allow them to express their creativity and individuality. While this pursuit is admirable, it can also lead to financial struggles if they prioritize purpose over financial security. Type 4s may find themselves in lower-paying or less stable professions, facing difficulties in achieving their desired level of financial abundance. Helping them find a balance between pursuing meaningful work and ensuring financial stability is crucial for their overall well-being.

Type 4 individuals are highly susceptible to comparison and envy, comparing themselves to others and longing for what they perceive as missing from their own lives. This can have significant implications for their financial decisions and behaviors. Type 4s may engage in impulse purchases or overspend to create an image that aligns with their idealized self. It is important to support Type 4s in cultivating self-compassion and understanding, helping them develop strategies to manage comparison and envy effectively, and make financial choices based on their own values and aspirations.

At the root of a Type 4 individual's financial journey lies a deep yearning for financial abundance and freedom. They desire the resources to fully express themselves and pursue their passions without restriction. However, their specific struggles and tendencies can pose challenges on this path. By identifying and addressing their financial challenges head-on, Type 4s can develop strategies and habits that support their quest for financial independence and genuine self-expression.

For Type 4 individuals, financial choices and possessions have a significant role in expressing their unique identity and individuality. They select investments, purchases, and experiences that reflect their values and aesthetic, creating an external reflection of their inner selves. While this can be a powerful tool for self-expression, it also has the potential to impact their financial well-being. Encouraging Type 4s to find a balance between financial expression and responsibility can help them build a solid foundation while honoring their authentic selves.

Type 4 individuals can overcome their financial struggles and tendencies by adopting creative approaches that support their unique needs. By embracing their emotional awareness, setting boundaries around their spending, and developing mindful practices, they can align their financial decisions with their values and aspirations. Moreover, cultivating gratitude and focusing on experiences rather than material possessions can bring a sense of fulfillment and reduce the need for excessive spending. The key is to find a balance between self-expression and financial responsibility, paving the way for financial growth and well-being.

Achieving financial stability and abundance while remaining true to oneself is within the reach of Type 4 individuals. By understanding their emotional relationship with money, reconciling their pursuit of authenticity with practical considerations, and developing strategies to manage comparison and envy, Type 4s can navigate their financial journey with confidence and purpose. With the right mindset and creative approaches, Type 4s can harness the power of their unique qualities and forge a path towards financial growth and balance.

Embracing Type 4's Strengths for Financial well-being

The Creative Mindset of Type 4 is a powerful asset when it comes to financial endeavors. Their innate ability to think outside the box and see the world through a creative lens can lead to lucrative careers or entrepreneurial ventures. Type 4s are often blessed with artistic talent, which can be transformed into a source of income. Many successful artists, writers, and musicians are Type 4s who have leveraged their creativity to achieve financial success. By tapping into their artistic talents and pursuing creative avenues for income generation, Type 4s can not only find financial fulfillment but also blend their work with their passions.

Type 4s also have a unique emotional depth that can be an asset in making sound financial decisions. Their ability to empathize with others and understand their emotional needs can make them excellent investors or financial planners. By recognizing this emotional intelligence and leaning into it, Type 4s can make investment choices that align with their values and have a positive impact on their financial well-being. They can avoid falling into the trap of solely chasing financial gains and instead focus on investments that resonate with their deeper purpose and values.

Developing a Unique Brand is another avenue for Type 4s to enhance their financial well-being. Type 4s value authenticity and self-expression. By harnessing their individuality, they can create a personal brand that stands out in the marketplace. This brand can reflect their unique talents, passions, and values, attracting a loyal customer base and creating opportunities for financial growth. Type 4s are known for their commitment to authenticity, and this authenticity can be a powerful tool in building a successful brand.

While Type 4s possess many strengths, it is also important to address the potential financial challenges they may face. Fluctuating income or difficulty with financial planning is not uncommon for Type 4s who often prioritize the present moment and their immediate emotional needs. To overcome these obstacles, Type 4s must develop strategies for managing their finances in a way that balances their desire for self-expression with practical considerations. Budgeting, investment planning, and seeking professional financial advice can provide the stability and security they need to pursue their passions while maintaining financial well-being.

Cultivating abundance through self-acceptance is vital for Type 4s to find financial success. By embracing their own uniqueness and accepting themselves fully, Type 4s can shift their mindset from scarcity to abundance. This shift opens up new possibilities and allows them to attract financial opportunities with a sense of confidence and authenticity.

Self-acceptance is intrinsically linked to financial success for Type 4s, as it enables them to tap into their strengths and pursue their goals with clarity and determination.

Type 4 individuals, with their deep desire for meaning and purpose, have an opportunity to align their financial pursuits with their deeper sense of purpose. By choosing careers or business opportunities that resonate with their values and passions, Type 4s can find fulfillment in their financial journey. When financial goals align with a greater purpose, they become more meaningful and motivating, driving Type 4s to achieve financial success while staying true to themselves.

Emotional intelligence plays a crucial role in financial decision-making, and Type 4s possess a natural emotional intelligence that can contribute to their financial well-being. By leveraging their intuitive abilities and emotional awareness, Type 4s can make wise financial decisions that align with their values and aspirations. Trusting their intuition and understanding the emotions that drive their financial choices empowers Type 4s to navigate their financial journey with clarity and conviction.

Type 4s often struggle to balance their idealism and creativity with practical financial strategies. It is important for them to find a delicate equilibrium between following their dreams and implementing practical financial plans. This balance allows Type 4s to pursue their passions while ensuring a stable and secure financial future. By acknowledging and managing both their idealistic tendencies and their practical needs, Type 4s can find financial success without compromising their individuality.

Creating a supportive network is crucial for Type 4s on their financial journey. Surrounding themselves with like-minded individuals who share their values and aspirations can provide guidance, encouragement, and a sense of community. This network can help Type 4s navigate challenges, share insights, and provide accountability. By building a supportive network, Type 4s can tap into collective wisdom, garner support, and propel themselves towards financial success.

Intuition and insight are innate gifts of Type 4s and should be utilized in their financial decision-making. Trusting their instincts and listening to their inner guidance can lead to wise financial choices and opportunities. By tapping into their intuitive abilities and embracing their innate insight, Type 4s can navigate the financial landscape with greater discernment and clarity.

To cultivate financial stability, Type 4s must embrace practical strategies such as budgeting, investment considerations, and long-term planning. By taking the necessary steps to build a solid financial foundation, Type 4s can achieve stability and security, enabling them to pursue their passions with peace of mind.

Embracing financial success is a crucial step for Type 4s. Often, their desire for authenticity may lead them to undervalue their accomplishments or shy away from celebrating their financial achievements. It is important for Type 4s to embrace their financial success and celebrate their achievements wholeheartedly. By acknowledging their financial growth and acknowledging their accomplishments, Type 4s create a positive mindset of abundance and attract further financial opportunities.

Embracing Type 4's strengths is essential for their financial well-being. By recognizing and harnessing their creative mindset, emotional depth, individuality, and emotional intelligence, Type 4s can forge a path towards financial growth and balance. By finding a delicate equilibrium between self-expression and financial responsibility, and cultivating a supportive network, Type 4s can overcome financial challenges and achieve both financial stability and abundance. Type 4s have unique gifts and perspectives that can be leveraged for their financial success, and it is my hope that this book provides them with the tools and insights necessary to embrace their strengths and embark on a fulfilling financial journey.

Practical Steps for Type 4's Financial Transformation

One of the challenges Type 4 individuals may face in achieving financial stability is their tendency to prioritize the present moment and their immediate emotional needs. Fluctuating income and difficulty with financial planning are not uncommon. To overcome these obstacles, Type 4s must create a solid financial foundation by implementing practical strategies such as budgeting and saving. By finding a balance between financial security and creative fulfillment, they can ensure that their financial journey supports their overall well-being.

Money holds a strong emotional resonance for Type 4s, often triggering feelings of scarcity or comparison. Managing these emotions is essential for a healthy relationship with money. Type 4s can cultivate a positive financial mindset by practicing self-awareness and self-love. By acknowledging and addressing their emotional patterns, they can develop tools for creating a healthy relationship with money based on their own unique needs and values.

Type 4s are naturally inclined towards creative pursuits and may be drawn to unconventional financial paths. While this creativity is a valuable asset, it is important for Type 4s to integrate practicality and long-term planning into their financial journey. By finding innovative solutions that align with their values and aspirations, they can create a financial path that supports both their individuality and their long-term financial well-being.

Valuing their financial worth can be a challenge for Type 4s. They may struggle with recognizing their own accomplishments and advocating for themselves and their financial goals. It is crucial for Type 4s to build confidence in their financial abilities and have a deep understanding of their value. By celebrating each small step towards financial growth, they can develop a sense of self-worth that strengthens their financial journey.

Type 4s have a unique opportunity to monetize their artistic talents and passions. By turning their creative hobbies into profitable ventures or side businesses, they can align their financial pursuits with their deepest passions. Thinking creatively about alternative income streams that align with their natural inclinations can open up new possibilities for financial success.

Fluctuating financial circumstances are not uncommon for Type 4s. Embracing a mindset of adaptability and viewing change as a creative opportunity can help them navigate these ups and downs. By building resilience and developing strategies for dealing with financial challenges and uncertainties, Type 4s can maintain their creative spirit while weathering any financial storms.

Type 4s are driven by their values and passions, and it is important for their financial choices to align with these principles. Seeking out socially responsible investing opportunities and practicing conscious consumerism can help Type 4s ensure that their financial portfolio reflects their authenticity. By investing in ways that support their values, they can find deeper meaning and purpose in their financial journey.

Type 4s must view financial wellness as part of their overall self-care journey. Integrating financial goals with emotional, physical, and spiritual well-being is essential for a balanced and fulfilling life. By recognizing the interconnectedness of different aspects of life and how they influence financial success, Type 4s can cultivate a holistic approach to their financial journey.

Building a network of mentors, advisors, and like-minded individuals who understand Type 4s' unique needs is crucial for their financial success. This network can provide guidance, encouragement, and accountability. By fostering open and honest communication about financial challenges and goals with loved ones, Type 4s can develop a strong support system that propels them towards their financial dreams.

As Type 4s embark on their financial transformation, it is vital to approach their journey with self-compassion and patience. Celebrating every small victory along the way and acknowledging their growth is essential for maintaining a positive mindset. This financial transformation is not just about money but also about self-expression and personal growth. By embracing their strengths, Type 4s can unleash their full financial potential and create a life that aligns with their true selves.

Chapter 6: The Investigator (Type 5)

The Investigator's Money Mindset

First and foremost, financial security is a key motivator for Type 5 individuals. They crave stability and independence, and having enough financial resources gives us a sense of control over our lives. This desire for security stems from our need to feel self-sufficient and protected. They understand that money provides a tangible means to ensure our basic needs are met and allows us the freedom to pursue our intellectual interests without the worry of financial burdens.

However, the fear of financial scarcity is an ever-present concern for investigators. They are constantly aware of the limited resources available in the world, and this fear drives our decision-making. It may manifest as hoarding, where they hold onto our money tightly and are reluctant to spend it, even on necessary expenses. This fear can also lead to excessive frugality, as they tirelessly search for ways to save and stretch our resources. It is important for us to recognize this fear and find a balance between saving for the future and enjoying the present.

A distinguishing characteristic of Type 5 individuals is our relentless pursuit of knowledge and information. Before making any financial decision, they delve deep into research, gathering facts, figures, and expert opinions. This dedication to acquiring knowledge can be both a blessing and a curse. On one hand, it equips us with the tools to make informed decisions and potentially avoid costly mistakes. On the other hand, it can lead to analysis paralysis, where they become overwhelmed by an excess of information and struggle to take action. Finding a balance between gathering knowledge and trusting our instincts is key to their financial success.

They prefer self-reliance when it comes to money matters. They trust their own abilities and are hesitant to rely on others, particularly when it comes to making financial decisions. They are often tempted to go it alone, believing that they have the expertise and knowledge to handle their finances independently. While self-reliance can be empowering, it is important for us to recognize that seeking advice from trusted financial professionals or mentors can provide valuable insights and guidance.

Despite their preference for self-reliance, investigators also fear being overwhelmed by financial responsibilities or controlled by others. This fear may hinder their willingness to engage with financial institutions, take risks, or seek the support and collaboration that is often beneficial in achieving financial growth. It is important for us to confront these fears and challenge the limiting beliefs that may be holding us back. By doing so, they can nurture a healthier relationship with money and open themselves up to new opportunities.

Finding a balance between financial autonomy and connection is also crucial for investigators. While they value independence, meaningful connections with others can provide valuable support and opportunities. Building a network of trusted individuals, seeking mentorship, and collaborating with others can lead to personal and financial growth while still honoring our core motivations and fears.

To foster financial growth and abundance, it is important for Type 5 individuals to embrace an abundance mindset. This involves challenging and reframing the limiting beliefs they may hold about money and wealth. By recognizing that resources are not limited and that opportunities for growth are abundant, they can shift their mindset from scarcity to abundance, opening themselves up to new possibilities.

Overcoming their aversion to risk-taking is another important aspect of the investigator's money mindset. they tend to be naturally cautious and hesitant to take risks, as they fear the potential for loss. However, calculated risks can lead to financial growth and new opportunities. Gradually expanding their comfort zones and developing a healthier relationship with risk-taking can ultimately serve us well in their financial journeys.

The investigator's money mindset is complex and deeply intertwined with their core motivations and fears. By understanding and embracing their unique money mindset, they can navigate financial decisions with greater confidence and purpose. It is important for investigators to strike a balance between financial security and enjoyment, leverage their natural inclination for acquiring knowledge, challenge limiting beliefs, seek support and collaboration, and embrace calculated risks. By doing so, they can achieve financial success and fulfillment while staying true to who they are as Type 5 individuals.

Financial Challenges Faced by Type 5

Type 5 individuals face a unique set of financial challenges that are deeply rooted in their core motivations and fears. One prominent challenge is their tendency to prioritize acquiring knowledge and information over accumulating wealth. As investigators, they have an insatiable thirst for learning and understanding, often diving deep into complex subjects that interest us. While this pursuit of knowledge can be fulfilling in many ways, it can also lead us to neglect important financial planning or investment opportunities. they may find themselves spending excessive time researching and analyzing financial options, but struggle to take decisive action or make concrete financial decisions.

Another challenge that Type 5 individuals face is difficulty in taking risks and making financial decisions. Their desire for security and understanding can make us naturally risk-averse, as they fear the potential consequences of making mistakes. This hesitancy can result in missed investment opportunities or limited financial growth. they may find themselves stuck in a state of analysis paralysis, where they become overwhelmed by an excess of information and struggle to take action. Finding a balance between gathering knowledge and trusting their instincts is key to their financial success.

They prefer self-reliance when it comes to money matters. They trust their own abilities and are hesitant to rely on others, particularly when it comes to making financial decisions. They are often tempted to go it alone, believing that they have the expertise and knowledge to handle their finances independently. While self-reliance can be empowering, it is important for us to recognize that seeking advice from trusted financial professionals or mentors can provide valuable insights and guidance.

Despite their preference for self-reliance, investigators also fear being overwhelmed by financial responsibilities or controlled by others. This fear may hinder their willingness to engage with financial institutions, take risks, or seek the support and collaboration that is often beneficial in achieving financial growth. It is important for us to confront these fears and challenge the limiting beliefs that may be holding us back. By doing so, they can nurture a healthier relationship with money and open themselves up to new opportunities.

Finding a balance between financial autonomy and connection is also crucial for investigators. While they value independence, meaningful connections with others can provide valuable support and opportunities. Building a network of trusted individuals, seeking mentorship, and collaborating with others can lead to personal and financial growth while still honoring their core motivations and fears.

To foster financial growth and abundance, it is important for Type 5 individuals to embrace an abundance mindset. This involves challenging and reframing the limiting beliefs they may hold about money and wealth. By recognizing that resources are not limited and that opportunities for growth are abundant, they can shift their mindset from scarcity to abundance, opening themselves up to new possibilities.

Overcoming their aversion to risk-taking is another important aspect of the investigator's money mindset. they tend to be naturally cautious and hesitant to take risks, as they fear the potential for loss. However, calculated risks can lead to financial growth and new opportunities. Gradually expanding their comfort zones and developing a healthier relationship with risk-taking can ultimately serve us well in their financial journeys.

The investigator's money mindset is complex and deeply intertwined with their core motivations and fears. By understanding and embracing their unique money mindset, they can navigate financial decisions with greater confidence and purpose. It is important for investigators to strike a balance between financial security and enjoyment, leverage their natural inclination for acquiring knowledge, challenge limiting beliefs, seek support and collaboration, and embrace calculated risks. By doing so, they can achieve financial success and fulfillment while staying true to who they are as Type 5 individuals.

Utilizing Type 5's Strengths for Financial Success

The systematic approach that Type 5 individuals naturally possess can be effectively utilized in financial planning. Their ability to organize and develop systems allows them to create a solid foundation for their financial journey. By setting clear goals, creating budgets, and implementing efficient processes,

Type 5 individuals can navigate their finances with a sense of control and direction.

One of the greatest strengths of Type 5 is their thirst for knowledge and research. When it comes to making informed and strategic financial decisions, this strength becomes invaluable. Type 5 individuals excel at gathering information, analyzing market trends, and understanding the intricacies of various investment options. By valuing knowledge and research, they can make sound financial choices that align with their long-term goals.

Type 5 individuals' analytical skills are a powerful tool when it comes to investing. Their ability to analyze data, evaluate risks, and make calculated decisions sets them apart in the financial arena. By leveraging their analytical talents, Type 5 individuals can excel in investment strategies and financial analysis, maximizing their returns while minimizing potential losses.

Type 5's cautious nature is often seen as a weakness, but when it comes to financial success, it can be a significant strength. Being naturally risk-averse, Type 5 individuals are prudent in assessing and managing risks. They have a knack for understanding the importance of diversification, insurance, and other risk mitigation techniques. By recognizing the importance of risk management, Type 5 individuals can effectively secure their wealth and protect it from potential threats.

While the analytical skills of Type 5 individuals are commendable, there lies a potential pitfall. Over-analyzing opportunities and succumbing to withdrawal tendencies can hinder financial progress. It is important for Type 5 individuals to strike a balance between analysis and action, recognizing that financial involvement is necessary for growth. By being mindful of these tendencies, Type 5 individuals can make decisions and take actions that are aligned with their financial goals.

Type 5 individuals excel at setting boundaries and protecting their resources. This strength is crucial in achieving financial security and growth. By establishing healthy financial boundaries, Type 5 individuals can safeguard their assets, prevent unnecessary expenditures, and ensure that they focus their resources on investments and opportunities that align with their long-term goals.

The creativity that Type 5 individuals possess can be harnessed in pursuing entrepreneurial ventures that are aligned with their interests and goals. Type 5 individuals have a unique ability to think outside the box, come up with innovative ideas, and solve complex problems. By leveraging their creativity, Type 5 individuals can identify lucrative business opportunities, create value for others, and achieve financial success through their entrepreneurial endeavors.

Type 5 individuals can cultivate financial confidence by continuously expanding their knowledge and expertise in money management. They have a natural inclination towards learning and accumulating knowledge, which can be channeled into acquiring a deep understanding of financial principles, strategies, and tools. By embracing lifelong learning, Type 5 individuals can boost their sense of confidence when it comes to making financial decisions.

Type 5 individuals excel at adapting to changing circumstances, and this flexibility is crucial in financial planning. The ability to adapt to new market conditions, investment opportunities, and financial trends can contribute to long-term financial success. By remaining open-minded and agile in their financial approach, Type 5 individuals can stay ahead of the curve and seize opportunities for growth.

While Type 5 individuals value independence, collaboration and seeking professional financial advice are essential for their financial growth. Building a network of trusted individuals, seeking mentorship, and collaborating with others can provide valuable support, guidance, and opportunities. By embracing collaboration and seeking professional advice when needed, Type 5 individuals can tap into knowledge and expertise outside of their own and enhance their financial decision-making.

Frugality is a natural inclination for Type 5 individuals, as they are mindful of conserving resources. While this strength is commendable, it is important for Type 5 individuals to balance frugality with investing in personal growth. By allocating resources towards their own education, skill development, and personal well-being, Type 5 individuals can enhance their value in the marketplace and increase their earning potential.

Type 5 individuals may have a tendency to fear scarcity and hold limiting beliefs about money and wealth. However, overcoming this fear and embracing an abundance mindset is crucial for financial success. By recognizing that resources and opportunities are abundant, Type 5 individuals can attract and seize financial opportunities, fostering a mindset that is conducive to wealth creation.

It is important for Type 5 individuals to nurture healthy relationships surrounding money. This includes setting clear communication with loved ones about financial goals, sharing financial responsibilities, and avoiding conflict around money matters. By nurturing healthy relationships, Type 5 individuals can create a supportive environment that promotes financial growth and stability.

Type 5 individuals possess unique strengths that can be harnessed for financial security and growth. By embracing a systematic approach to financial planning, valuing knowledge and research, leveraging analytical skills, recognizing the importance of risk management, being mindful of over-analyzing tendencies, setting healthy financial boundaries, harnessing creativity in entrepreneurial ventures, cultivating financial confidence, embracing flexibility and adaptability, seeking collaboration and professional advice, balancing frugality with personal growth, overcoming fear of scarcity, and nurturing healthy relationships around money, Type 5 individuals can achieve lasting financial success. It is by embracing and harnessing their unique strengths that Type 5 individuals can navigate the world of money with confidence, purpose, and fulfillment.

Practical Strategies for Type 5's Financial

Empowerment

Type 5 individuals are known for their analytical nature and cautious approach to money. They value knowledge and have a strong desire for financial security and independence. To empower yourself financially, it is crucial to leverage these strengths and implement practical strategies tailored to your needs.

First and foremost, financial education plays a significant role in Type 5 individuals' journey towards financial empowerment. Your thirst for knowledge can be harnessed to make informed financial decisions. Invest time in reading books, attending seminars, and taking courses that enhance your financial literacy. The more you understand about money management, investing, and financial planning, the better equipped you will be to create a solid financial foundation.

Type 5 individuals often have a natural inclination towards frugality and cautious spending. While budgeting is important for financial success, it is essential to strike a balance. Create a budget that aligns with your financial goals while still allowing for occasional indulgences. This way, you can enjoy your hard-earned money without compromising your long-term financial security.

Saving and investing are integral parts of financial empowerment for Type 5 individuals. With a strong desire for financial security, saving becomes a priority. Set specific savings goals and automate your savings to ensure consistency. Additionally, explore investment options that align with your risk tolerance and long-term goals. Consider diversifying your investments to mitigate risk and seek professional advice when needed.

Type 5 individuals often face challenges in earning income and advancing professionally due to their introverted nature and preference for independent work. To overcome these challenges, it is important to find a balance between financial growth and personal fulfillment. Seek opportunities that align with your interests and values while also providing financial stability. Consider leveraging your analytical skills in fields such as research, consulting, or entrepreneurship where you can have control over your financial destiny.

Maintaining balance is crucial for Type 5 individuals. While financial security and independence are important, it is equally important to prioritize personal fulfillment and well-being. Regularly assess your priorities and ensure you are dedicating time, energy, and resources to activities that bring you joy and personal growth. Remember that true financial empowerment is about achieving both financial success and a fulfilling life.

Type 5 individuals' desire for knowledge and competence should guide their financial decision-making. While you have strengths in analysis and research, it is important to seek professional financial advice when needed. Professionals can provide insights and guidance tailored to your unique needs and goals. Recognize that seeking advice is a sign of intelligence and is crucial for making well-informed financial decisions.

Leveraging your analytical skills and attention to detail can optimize your financial strategies. Conduct thorough research, analyze different options, and stay informed about financial trends and strategies. Make informed decisions based on your analysis, and trust in your abilities to navigate the complex world of finance.

Be mindful of overthinking and analysis paralysis. While it is important to be thorough in your research and decision-making, avoid getting stuck in a cycle of endless analysis. Recognize when it is time to take action and make progress towards your financial goals. Remember that mistakes and setbacks are part of the journey, and it is through taking action that true learning and growth occur.

Setting achievable and measurable financial goals is crucial for Type 5 individuals. Break down your long-term goals into smaller milestones and track your progress. Celebrate your achievements along the way and adjust your strategies as necessary. By setting clear goals and monitoring your progress, you can stay motivated and focused on your financial empowerment.

Seeking financial advice and guidance can be challenging for Type 5 individuals who value independence. However, it is essential to find professionals who understand your unique needs and can provide relevant advice. Look for trusted financial advisors or join financial communities where you can connect with like-minded individuals and gain valuable insights and opportunities.

THE ENNEAGRAM AND MONEY

Self-awareness is key in your financial journey. Understand your motivations and fears related to money, as this self-awareness can guide your financial decision-making. Recognize any limiting beliefs or emotional barriers that may be holding you back from achieving your full financial potential. By addressing these inner obstacles, you can overcome them and move closer to financial empowerment.

To continuously grow in your financial journey, engage in continuous learning. Stay updated on financial trends, strategies, and tools. Attend seminars, read financial publications, and join communities where you can learn from others' experiences. Embrace a growth mindset and always be open to expanding your knowledge and skills.

Collaboration and networking can also play a significant role in your financial success. Connect with like-minded individuals and professionals, as they can provide valuable insights and opportunities. Seek collaborative projects, partnerships, or mentorship that can enhance your financial growth. By joining forces with others, you can leverage collective knowledge and expertise to achieve greater financial empowerment.

Periodic review and adjustment of your financial strategies is crucial for continued progress. As circumstances change, evaluate and modify your financial plans accordingly. Regularly review your budget, investments, and goals to ensure they align with your current situation and long-term objectives. By staying proactive and adaptable, you can navigate changing financial landscapes and maintain a sense of empowerment.

Finally, I want to offer encouragement and support for your financial journey. Embracing financial empowerment can have a profound impact on your overall well-being and personal growth. By leveraging your unique strengths, embracing knowledge, setting clear goals, balancing frugality with personal growth, seeking professional advice, and nurturing healthy relationships around money, you can achieve lasting financial success. Believe in yourself, stay committed to your goals, and never underestimate the power of your financial potential.

Chapter 7: The Loyalist (Type 6)

The Loyalist's Money Mentality

As I delved deeper into the Enneagram and its relationship with money, I discovered the fascinating world of the loyalist personality type, also known as Type 6. Type 6 individuals, driven by their core fear of uncertainty, navigate the financial landscape with a distinct mindset and set of motivations. Understanding their money mentality is crucial for both Type 6 individuals themselves and those seeking to build strong financial relationships with them.

At the heart of Type 6 individuals lies a fear that permeates their every decision—the fear of uncertainty. This fear shapes their financial choices, leading them to prioritize stability and security above all else. For a loyalist, the thought of not knowing what the future holds can be paralyzing. As a result, they are often drawn to careers that offer a sense of stability, a steady paycheck, and job security. They tend to value savings and prefer the peace of mind that comes with having a financial safety net. Additionally, Type 6 individuals may be more risk-averse than other types, preferring to take calculated steps rather than diving headfirst into uncertain investments.

Loyalty and trust are the pillars that hold the loyalist's world together. Type 6 individuals crave a sense of belonging and surround themselves with dependable relationships and institutions. When it comes to finances, this need for loyalty and trust plays a significant role. They tend to seek out financial institutions and advisors known for their stability and reliability, seeing them as a source of reassurance. For a loyalist, the thought of placing their hard-earned money into the hands of anyone they can't trust is unfathomable. Consequently, they may be cautious with investments and prefer the comfort of what is tried and tested.

Type 6 individuals are known for their preparedness and ability to anticipate potential dangers or crises. This mindset extends to their financial choices as well. Building emergency funds and having multiple income streams are common tactics employed by the loyalist to combat their fear of uncertainty. They understand that financial security is an essential factor in alleviating their anxieties. By developing a safety net, Type 6 individuals create a sense of stability that allows them to face the unknown with more confidence.

For Type 6 individuals, decision-making can be a daunting task. The fear of making the wrong choice often leads to anxiety and paralysis. This struggle is evident in their financial choices as well. They may find it challenging to commit to significant financial decisions, be it investing in stocks or purchasing a home. The loyalist weighs every possible outcome, analyzing the pros and cons of each path, often resulting in hesitation and missed opportunities. Overcoming this challenges Type 6 individuals to embrace a more assertive financial approach, taking calculated risks and trusting their own judgment.

The loyalist craves a community of like-minded individuals, a safe haven where they can find support and reassurance. In their financial lives, Type 6 individuals often seek out trusted friends, family members, or mentors for advice and guidance. Combining the trust placed in these relationships with their inherent loyalty, loyalists find comfort in the company of those who share their financial values and goals. By connecting with others on a financial level, Type 6 individuals can gain new insights and perspectives, helping them navigate their money mentality with more confidence.

To break free from fear-based financial patterns, Type 6 individuals must consciously disrupt their mental narratives. Building trust in the decision-making process is crucial, as is understanding that calculated risks can lead to growth and financial success. Learning to strike a balance between security and growth is the key to overcoming their fear of uncertainty. By gradually expanding their comfort zone and challenging themselves to step outside their predetermined boundaries, Type 6 individuals can unlock newfound financial opportunities.

Despite their fear of uncertainty, Type 6 individuals possess a unique set of strengths and opportunities when it comes to their finances. Their emphasis on stability and preparedness can act as a foundation for long-term financial success. By harnessing their loyalty and meticulousness, the loyalist can build strong financial relationships and make informed decisions. However, it is essential to recognize that growth exists beyond their comfort zone. Embracing new experiences and perspectives can open the door to uncharted financial opportunities that align with their deepest desires.

Throughout my journey of exploring the Enneagram and money, I have encountered countless stories of Type 6 individuals and their financial journeys. These real-life examples serve as a testament to the power of understanding one's money mentality. From a loyalist who transformed their fear of uncertainty into a thriving entrepreneurship venture to another who learned to make confident investment decisions despite their initial hesitations, the stories provide invaluable insights and inspiration. By learning from the experiences of others, Type 6 individuals can find solace in knowing that they are not alone in their financial struggles and that growth is always possible.

Understanding the loyalist's money mentality is a transformative step in developing a healthy and balanced relationship with money. By recognizing and addressing their core fears and motivations, Type 6 individuals can unleash their full financial potential and find peace amidst the unpredictability of life. Throughout this chapter, they have explored the various facets of the loyalist's money mentality, from their fear of uncertainty to their desire for stability and trust. In the following chapters, they will delve deeper into the remaining Enneagram types, unraveling the unique money mentalities that drive their financial choices. I invite you to continue exploring the Enneagram and its profound impact on their financial dynamics as they embark on this transformative journey together.

Financial Struggles of Type 6

The fears and anxieties that drive Type 6 individuals' financial decisions and behaviors, including their fear of scarcity and lack of financial security. As a loyalist, Type 6 individuals constantly strive for security and stability in all aspects of their lives, including their finances. Their fear of scarcity and lack of financial security drives them to prioritize saving and building emergency funds. They often worry about not having enough money to sustain themselves and their loved ones in times of crisis. This fear can lead to a scarcity mindset and a deep-rooted belief that there will never be enough. The challenge for Type 6 individuals lies in finding a balance between their need for security and the potential for financial growth.

The tendency of Type 6 individuals to be risk-averse when it comes to investing and taking financial risks, and strategies for helping them overcome this mindset to achieve financial growth. Type 6 individuals are naturally risk-averse and cautious, which can inhibit their ability to take financial risks and seize investment opportunities. Their fear of making the wrong decision often leads them to avoid investing altogether or to choose conservative investment options with minimal potential for growth. To break free from this mindset, Type 6 individuals need to cultivate trust in themselves and the decision-making process. They can start by educating themselves about different investment strategies and gradually exposing themselves to calculated risks. Working with a financial advisor who understands their risk tolerance and can guide them in making informed investment decisions can also be beneficial.

The struggle of Type 6 individuals to trust financial institutions and authority figures, and tips for building trust and finding reliable financial advice. Type 6 individuals have a natural skepticism towards authority figures and financial institutions. They may struggle to trust financial advisors, banks, or any authority figure when it comes to their money. This mistrust can hinder their financial growth and lead to missed opportunities. To overcome this challenge, Type 6 individuals can approach the task of finding reliable financial advice with caution. They can conduct thorough research, seek recommendations from trusted friends or family members, and interview potential advisors to ensure they feel a sense of trust before making a commitment. Building a relationship with a financial advisor based on transparency, open communication, and shared values can help Type 6 individuals develop trust over time.

The difficulty for Type 6 individuals to make decisions when it comes to financial planning and investments, and strategies to help them navigate this challenge. Decision-making can be a struggle for Type 6 individuals due to their fear of making the wrong choice. This fear can often result in analysis paralysis, where they find themselves unable to make a decision. To overcome this challenge, Type 6 individuals can start by acknowledging that no decision is perfect and that mistakes are an inevitable part of the learning process. They can seek support and guidance from trusted individuals or professionals to help them weigh the pros and cons of different options. Developing a decision-making framework that aligns with their values and financial goals can also provide a sense of structure and confidence in their decision-making process.

The tendency for Type 6 individuals to prioritize financial stability over personal fulfillment, and advice on finding a balance between security and pursuing their passions. As loyalists, Type 6 individuals often prioritize financial stability over personal fulfillment. They may settle for secure but unfulfilling jobs or careers due to their fear of financial insecurity. Finding a balance between security and pursuing their passions requires Type 6 individuals to identify their core values and align their financial choices with those values. They can explore alternative income sources or side hustles that provide both financial stability and a sense of fulfillment. It is essential for Type 6 individuals to recognize that pursuing their passions can also lead to long-term financial success and security.

Harnessing Type 6's Strengths for Financial well-being

One of the most prominent strengths of Type 6 individuals when it comes to finances is their unwavering loyalty. This loyalty extends not only to their relationships but also to their financial stability. Type 6 individuals have a remarkable tendency to prioritize and work towards financial security. As a result, they are more likely to engage in long-term financial planning and develop resilience in the face of economic uncertainties. By harnessing this loyalty, Type 6 individuals can lay a strong foundation for a secure financial future.

Type 6 individuals are known for their analytical and meticulous approach to decision-making. When it comes to financial choices, this thoroughness can be a significant asset. Type 6 individuals carefully consider potential risks and rewards, conducting extensive research before making financial decisions. By evaluating all angles and weighing the pros and cons, they make prudent choices that minimize potential pitfalls. This methodical approach helps Type 6 individuals avoid impulsive and ill-informed financial decisions, ultimately leading to greater financial well-being.

One of the remarkable strengths of Type 6 individuals is their ability to anticipate and prepare for potential challenges. This preparedness, rooted in their natural inclination towards risk aversion, enables them to develop contingency plans and emergency funds. Consequently, Type 6 individuals derive a sense of security and stability even during uncertain times. Harnessing this natural inclination for preparedness allows them to navigate financial challenges with greater ease, providing a solid foundation for their financial well-being.

Type 6 individuals possess a natural caution and skepticism, which can be a valuable strength when it comes to managing finances. This prudence enables them to conduct thorough research and take calculated risks. By carefully evaluating the potential rewards and risks of investments or financial decisions, Type 6 individuals minimize the chances of detrimental financial loss. Their cautious approach ensures that they make well-informed choices and protect their financial interests in the long run.

Type 6 individuals have a strong desire to seek information and knowledge to enhance their decision-making process. When it comes to financial matters, this diligence in educating themselves can be particularly beneficial. Type 6 individuals are committed to understanding the intricacies of personal finance, staying updated on market trends, and exploring various investment strategies. By continuously expanding their financial knowledge, Type 6 individuals make informed decisions that align with their financial goals, increasing their chances of long-term financial success.

Type 6 individuals have a remarkable capacity to remain resilient in the face of financial challenges or setbacks. Their ability to adapt and pivot their financial strategies in response to changing circumstances is a testament to their strength and determination. Type 6 individuals can swiftly adjust their financial plans, seeking alternative income sources or exploring new opportunities when faced with adversity. This resilience ensures that they remain on track towards their financial goals, even in the face of unexpected obstacles.

While Type 6 individuals prioritize security and stability, they also possess an openness to financial growth and opportunity. This balanced approach allows them to find a middle ground between caution and taking calculated financial risks. By recognizing the importance of stepping out of their comfort zone while still safeguarding their financial interests, Type 6 individuals can seize opportunities for growth and advancement while maintaining a sense of security.

Type 6 individuals have a natural inclination to consider the greater good and prioritize collective well-being in their financial decisions. This community-oriented approach often leads them to make socially responsible financial choices, ensuring that their money positively impacts not only their own lives but also those around them. By harnessing this inclination, Type 6 individuals can find a sense of fulfillment in contributing to the community and promote financial well-being on a broader scale.

Type 6 individuals may struggle to trust financial institutions and authority figures due to their inherent skepticism. However, they can leverage their trust and reliance on trusted advisors as a strength in managing their finances. By seeking guidance and support from reputable financial professionals, Type 6 individuals gain access to well-informed advice that aligns with their risk tolerance and financial goals. Building a relationship based on transparency and shared values helps foster trust over time, enabling Type 6 individuals to make confident and informed financial decisions.

Type 6 individuals possess an innate sense of intuition when it comes to financial matters. Despite their tendency towards thorough analysis, they also have the ability to trust their gut feelings and make intuitive decisions. By combining their analytical thinking with their financial intuition, Type 6 individuals can navigate complex financial situations confidently and achieve successful outcomes.

Type 6 individuals' reflective and introspective nature is a valuable asset when it comes to financial growth. They engage in self-reflection to evaluate their financial strategies, adapt their approaches, and seek continuous improvement. This introspective nature helps Type 6 individuals identify their financial strengths and weaknesses, allowing them to make necessary adjustments and pursue long-term financial success.

Type 6 individuals possess a remarkable ability to strike a balance between individual financial independence and the importance of relying on trusted confidants. They understand the value of building a support network that fosters financial well-being, offering a sense of security and collaboration. By cultivating relationships with reliable partners who share their financial goals and values, Type 6 individuals leverage their interdependence to achieve greater financial stability and success.

Financial setbacks are inevitable, but Type 6 individuals have a unique ability to bounce back in the face of adversity. They learn from their failures, adapt their strategies, and maintain a positive outlook. This resilient approach enables them to persevere and overcome obstacles, ultimately leading to greater financial stability and success.

Type 6 individuals have a natural inclination to collaborate and form partnerships in their financial endeavors. They recognize the benefits of shared resources, knowledge exchange, and increased opportunities for financial growth. By fostering collaboration with like-minded individuals, Type 6 individuals enhance their financial prospects and achieve their goals more effectively.

Type 6 individuals possess inherent flexibility and adaptability when it comes to financial matters. They understand the importance of adjusting their financial strategies and adapting to changing circumstances. By embracing flexibility, Type 6 individuals ensure their financial resilience and navigate various financial challenges with grace and success.

The decision-making process of Type 6 individuals regarding finances is characterized by a meticulous and thoughtful approach. They weigh pros and cons, seek multiple perspectives, and consider various scenarios before making financial choices. This well-rounded decision-making process enables Type 6 individuals to make informed decisions and align their financial actions with their values and goals.

Type 6 individuals approach financial planning with mindfulness and a holistic view. They consider not only short-term goals but also long-term aspirations, ensuring a balanced and comprehensive financial strategy. By bringing mindfulness to their financial planning process, Type 6 individuals actively engage with their financial goals, enhancing their chances of long-term success and fulfillment.

Harnessing the strengths of Type 6 individuals leads to increased financial confidence and empowerment. By understanding and utilizing their unique qualities, Type 6 individuals navigate financial challenges with resilience and success. This newfound confidence empowers them to take control of their finances, make informed decisions, and embrace financial opportunities that align with their goals and values.

While harnessing their strengths is crucial for Type 6 individuals, ongoing personal and financial growth remain essential. By recognizing the importance of continuous improvement, Type 6 individuals are motivated to expand their financial knowledge, adapt their strategies, and seek new opportunities for growth. This commitment to growth enables Type 6 individuals to achieve and maintain long-term financial well-being.

Actionable Steps for Type 6's Financial Growth

1. Acknowledge and Address Fear and Anxiety: Type 6 individuals need to recognize and confront their anxieties and fears around money. This can be done through self-reflection, therapy, or support groups. By acknowledging and addressing these emotions, Type 6 individuals can take steps towards cultivating a more positive and confident financial mindset.

2. Create a Financial Vision: Type 6 individuals should take time to reflect on their financial goals and aspirations. This involves envisioning their ideal financial future and identifying what steps need to be taken to achieve it. By setting clear and specific goals, Type 6 individuals can focus their efforts and stay motivated throughout their financial journey.

3. Develop a Budget: Type 6 individuals should create a budget that aligns with their need for security and stability. This involves tracking expenses, prioritizing savings, and setting aside funds for unexpected expenses. Creating a budget allows Type 6 individuals to have a clear understanding of their

financial situation and make informed decisions about how to allocate their resources.

4. Build an Emergency Fund: Type 6 individuals should prioritize building an emergency fund to protect themselves from unforeseen financial challenges. This involves setting aside a certain percentage of their income each month and establishing a target amount to strive for. An emergency fund provides peace of mind and serves as a safety net during times of uncertainty.

5. Seek Professional Financial Advice: Type 6 individuals can benefit greatly from seeking guidance from financial professionals. This involves finding a trustworthy financial advisor who understands their unique needs and anxieties. A professional can help Type 6 individuals navigate complex financial decisions, provide reassurance, and offer strategies for long-term financial success.

6. Diversify Investments: Type 6 individuals should consider diversifying their investments to mitigate risk and maximize returns. This involves spreading investments across different asset classes, industries, or geographical locations. Diversification allows Type 6 individuals to protect their financial interests and potentially increase their wealth over time.

7. Cultivate a Supportive Financial Community: Type 6 individuals should seek out a supportive community of like-minded individuals who share similar financial goals and values. This can be done through joining financial support

groups, attending workshops or seminars, or participating in online forums. By surrounding themselves with people who understand and support their financial journey, Type 6 individuals can find comfort, motivation, and guidance along the way.

8. Practice Self-Reflection and Mindfulness: Type 6 individuals should regularly engage in self-reflection and mindfulness exercises to stay grounded and focused on their financial goals. This can involve journaling, meditation, or seeking moments of solitude. By practicing self-reflection and mindfulness, Type 6 individuals can make more intentional financial decisions and avoid impulsive or fear-driven choices.

9. Take Calculated Risks: Type 6 individuals should be open to taking calculated risks when it comes to their finances. This involves carefully assessing potential rewards and risks before making investment decisions or pursuing new financial opportunities. By stepping out of their comfort zone and embracing calculated risks, Type 6 individuals can create opportunities for financial growth and expansion.

10. Celebrate Financial Milestones: Type 6 individuals should celebrate their financial milestones to stay motivated and foster a positive relationship with money. This involves acknowledging and rewarding themselves for achieving savings goals, paying off debts, or reaching investment milestones. Celebrating financial milestones can act as a reinforcement of their progress and encourage continued financial growth.

Overall, Type 6 individuals have the potential to achieve financial well-being by harnessing their strengths, addressing their fears and anxieties, and implementing actionable steps towards their financial goals. With commitment, persistence, and a supportive network, Type 6 individuals can navigate the complexities of money with confidence, leading to a life of financial security and peace of mind.

Chapter 8: The Enthusiast (Type 7)

The Enthusiast's Relationship With Money

The driving force behind a Type 7 individual's financial choices is their relentless pursuit of happiness and fulfillment. They have an insatiable desire for new experiences and an ingrained fear of missing out. This combination can greatly impact their financial decisions, often causing them to prioritize short-term pleasure over long-term financial stability.

Due to their strong aversion to boredom and routine, impulsive spending becomes a common occurrence for Type 7 individuals. They struggle to save, constantly chasing after immediate gratification to avoid the possibility of missing out on opportunities and experiences. This perpetual desire for instant happiness can create challenges when it comes to building long-term financial security.

Commitment, or rather the fear of being tied down, is another aspect that significantly influences the financial behavior of Type 7 individuals. This fear manifests not only in relationships but also in matters of money. They may be reluctant to invest in long-term financial goals or make firm financial decisions, fearing that it will restrict their freedom to explore new opportunities.

These unique financial challenges Type 7 individuals face can contribute to a cycle of financial instability and even debt. Their relentless pursuit of new experiences can lead them to overextend themselves financially, fueling their fear of missing out even further.

To break this cycle, it is crucial for Type 7 individuals to find fulfillment while maintaining balance and focus in their financial lives.

One effective strategy for achieving financial fulfillment is to establish clear financial goals and create a budget that allows for both enjoyment and long-term stability. By setting goals and prioritizing their spending based on those objectives, Type 7 individuals can ensure that they are making intentional choices that align with their desires for experiences and their need for financial health.

Moreover, it is vital for Type 7 individuals to find fulfillment in experiences that do not require excessive spending. Engaging in activities and hobbies that align with their values and provide long-term satisfaction can help quell the constant urge for instant gratification.

The fear of missing out can be a pervasive presence in the lives of Type 7 individuals. To reduce its impact, it is important for them to embrace the present moment and practice gratitude for what they already have. By focusing on the blessings that surround them, they can minimize their fear of missing out and find contentment in the here and now.

Leveraging their natural ability to adapt and be resourceful is another way for Type 7 individuals to overcome financial challenges. Their optimistic outlook and flexibility can provide an advantage in finding creative solutions and seizing new opportunities. However, it's important for them to approach financial decisions with caution and optimism, balancing their enthusiasm with a realistic evaluation of potential risks.

Seeking support and guidance is crucial for Type 7 individuals to navigate the complexities of finance. Working with a financial advisor or seeking out resources that align with their values can help them create a balanced and secure financial future. By seeking guidance, they can harness their enthusiasm and optimism while making informed financial choices.

In summary, understanding the core motivations and fears that influence Type 7 individuals' financial decisions is essential for establishing a healthy relationship with money. By embracing their enthusiasm and optimism, while intentionally and prudently making financial choices, Type 7 individuals can create a fulfilling life that aligns with their values and ensures long-term financial well-being.

Financial Challenges Faced by Type 7

Type 7 individuals are known for their fear of missing out on exciting experiences. Their optimistic and adventurous nature often compels them to seek new opportunities and indulge in various experiences. While this mindset can bring excitement and joy to their lives, it can also pose challenges when it comes to managing finances.

Type 7 individuals may find themselves succumbing to impulsive spending, chasing after every new and thrilling experience that captures their fancy. They may struggle to prioritize their financial goals, as the fear of missing out intensifies their desire to seize every opportunity. This can lead to a lack of focus and commitment when it comes to long-term financial planning.

Furthermore, the fear of missing out can also blind Type 7 individuals to the potential consequences of their impulsive spending. They may fail to recognize the long-term impact of their financial decisions, which can result in personal debt and financial instability.

Another challenge that Type 7 individuals face is their tendency to use excessive spending or financial distractions as a way to avoid uncomfortable emotions. The enthusiastic and adventurous nature of Type 7 individuals often makes them uncomfortable with negative emotions or experiences. To cope with these feelings, they may turn to instant gratification through spending, hoping to escape from any unpleasant emotions.

However, this behavior can have a detrimental effect on their overall financial well-being. By avoiding their emotions through financial distractions, such as excessive spending or constantly seeking new experiences, Type 7 individuals may overlook the importance of saving, investing, and planning for their future financial security.

To overcome this challenge, Type 7 individuals need to develop healthier coping mechanisms and ways to deal with uncomfortable emotions. They can engage in mindfulness practices, seek therapy, or explore hobbies and activities that provide emotional fulfillment without solely relying on financial distractions.

Type 7 individuals may find it challenging to stay focused and committed to their long-term financial goals. Their enthusiasm for new opportunities and experiences can easily divert their attention, making it difficult to stay on track with financial planning and stability.

To overcome this challenge, Type 7 individuals can benefit from developing strategies that help them maintain focus and commitment. They can set specific and achievable financial goals, break them down into smaller milestones, and regularly review their progress. Additionally, seeking support from trusted friends, family members, or financial advisors can provide accountability and guidance to stay on track.

Type 7 individuals often crave immediate gratification, seeking out experiences that bring them instant joy and excitement. However, this desire for short-term gratification can lead to a cycle of constantly chasing after the next thrilling experience, without considering its long-term impact on their financial well-being.

This cycle of short-term gratification can result in a pattern of accumulating debt or living paycheck to paycheck, as Type 7 individuals struggle to strike a balance between enjoying the present and ensuring future financial stability.

To break this cycle, Type 7 individuals need to cultivate patience and the ability to delay gratification. They can practice mindfulness and reflection before making impulsive financial decisions, evaluating whether the desired experience truly aligns with their long-term financial goals.

Linked to the cycle of short-term gratification is Type 7 individuals' discomfort with delayed gratification. The idea of waiting and saving for future financial goals can feel constricting and restricting, provoking anxiety and restlessness. As a result, Type 7 individuals may struggle to save and invest for their future financial security.

To overcome this challenge, Type 7 individuals can shift their mindset and prioritize the importance of future financial stability. They can practice reframing delayed gratification as a necessary step towards achieving their long-term goals and cultivate a sense of satisfaction in the act of saving and investing.

Underlying many of the financial behaviors of Type 7 individuals is the fear of feeling trapped or restricted. This fear can manifest in various ways when it comes to their finances. They may avoid making financial commitments, such as investments or long-term savings plans, out of fear that it will limit their freedom and ability to explore new opportunities.

To overcome this fear, Type 7 individuals need to challenge their beliefs and recognize that financial commitments can actually provide a sense of stability, security, and freedom in the long run. By reframing their perspective, they can embrace financial commitments as a means to create a solid foundation that allows them to continue to explore and enjoy new experiences.

Type 7 individuals are often drawn to new financial opportunities and may have a propensity for risk-taking. Their optimistic outlook and adaptability may make them more willing to seize new opportunities without fully evaluating the potential risks involved.

To strike a balance between their natural enthusiasm and financial prudence, Type 7 individuals need to approach financial decisions with caution and informed decision-making. They can seek advice from financial professionals who specialize in evaluating risk and return, and develop a thorough understanding of the potential rewards and consequences before committing to any financial opportunity.

Type 7 individuals may have a tendency to seek quick-fix solutions to their financial challenges. Instead of engaging in thoughtful consideration and long-term planning, they may make impulsive financial decisions that only provide temporary relief.

To break free from this cycle, Type 7 individuals can adopt a more deliberate approach to their financial decision-making. They can take the time to thoroughly research and evaluate various options before making a commitment. Creating a financial plan that aligns with their long-term goals and seeking advice from financial professionals can also help promote more thoughtful consideration in their financial decision-making process.

One of the key strategies for Type 7 individuals to achieve financial fulfillment is to establish clear financial goals and create a budget that allows for both enjoyment and long-term stability. By setting goals and prioritizing their spending based on those objectives, Type 7 individuals can ensure that they are making intentional choices that align with their desires for experiences and their need for financial health.

Moreover, it is vital for Type 7 individuals to find fulfillment in experiences that do not require excessive spending. Engaging in activities and hobbies that align with their values and provide long-term satisfaction can help quell the constant urge for instant gratification.

The fear of missing out can be a pervasive presence in the lives of Type 7 individuals. To reduce its impact, it is important for them to embrace the present moment and practice gratitude for what they already have. By focusing on the blessings that surround them, they can minimize their fear of missing out and find contentment in the here and now.

Leveraging their natural ability to adapt and be resourceful is another way for Type 7 individuals to overcome financial challenges. Their optimistic outlook and flexibility can provide an advantage in finding creative solutions and seizing new opportunities. However, it's important for them to approach financial decisions with caution and optimism, balancing their enthusiasm with a realistic evaluation of potential risks.

Seeking support and guidance is crucial for Type 7 individuals to navigate the complexities of finance. Working with a financial advisor or seeking out resources that align with their values can help them create a balanced and secure financial future. By seeking guidance, they can harness their enthusiasm and optimism while making informed financial choices.

In summary, understanding the core motivations and fears that influence Type 7 individuals' financial decisions is essential for establishing a healthy relationship with money. By embracing their enthusiasm and optimism while intentionally and prudently making financial choices, Type 7 individuals can create a fulfilling life that aligns with their values and ensures long-term financial well-being.

Turning the page to the next chapter, they will explore the financial mindset and behaviors of Type 8 individuals. This chapter will delve into their unique approach to money and provide insights on how they can achieve financial empowerment and growth. By understanding the financial dynamics of each Enneagram type, they can further enhance our understanding of our own financial patterns and behaviors, and ultimately establish a healthier relationship with money.

Leveraging Type 7's Strengths for Financial Success

Type 7 individuals possess a number of inherent strengths that, when harnessed effectively, can lead to great financial success and fulfillment. Their adventurous nature, optimism, adaptability, enthusiasm, multitasking abilities, resilience, creativity, focus, and ability to find joy in abundance all contribute to their potential for financial prosperity. By understanding and leveraging these qualities, Type 7 individuals can navigate the world of finance with confidence and achieve their financial goals.

First and foremost, Type 7 individuals are known for their adventurous nature. They possess a deep curiosity and eagerness for new experiences. This sense of adventure can be harnessed to discover new opportunities for financial growth and success. Their willingness to explore uncharted territories and take risks can lead to innovative business ventures or investments that yield significant returns. By embracing their natural inclination for exploration, Type 7 individuals can uncover hidden gems in the financial landscape and make bold moves that propel them towards financial fulfillment.

Type 7 individuals also possess a remarkable level of optimism. They have a natural tendency to see the glass as half full and approach life with a positive mindset. This optimism plays a crucial role in their financial success, as it allows them to overcome challenges and maintain motivation during difficult times. Rather than being discouraged by setbacks, Type 7 individuals view them as opportunities for growth and learning. This unwavering belief in their ability to overcome obstacles serves as a driving force in their pursuit of financial success.

Flexibility and adaptability are two other key strengths exhibited by Type 7 individuals. They possess the ability to effortlessly navigate different situations and adapt to changing circumstances. In the realm of finance, this skill becomes invaluable. Financial landscapes are constantly evolving, and being able to adapt quickly to market shifts and changes in opportunities is essential. Type 7 individuals can seize profitable opportunities and adjust their strategies accordingly, ensuring that they stay ahead of the game and make the most out of every financial situation.

One of the most captivating qualities of Type 7 individuals is their infectious enthusiasm. Their genuine excitement for what they do is magnetic and can attract potential clients and customers to their financial endeavors. This enthusiasm, coupled with their inherent creativity and ability to generate out-of-the-box ideas, enables them to develop innovative financial strategies and business concepts that stand out in a crowded market. By infusing their passion and creativity into their financial endeavors, Type 7 individuals can differentiate themselves and attract success.

Type 7 individuals also possess a natural talent for multitasking. They excel at juggling multiple projects and responsibilities simultaneously. In the context of finance, this skill becomes highly relevant for effective financial planning. They can manage their finances, investments, and business ventures with ease, ensuring that no aspect is overlooked or neglected. This ability to multitask allows Type 7 individuals to stay organized and on top of their financial affairs, maximizing their chances of success.

Additionally, Type 7 individuals are incredibly resilient. They have an innate ability to bounce back from setbacks and failures. In the world of finance where risks are inherent, this resilience becomes a paramount quality. Type 7 individuals can learn from their mistakes, draw lessons from their failures, and make better financial decisions in the future. Rather than being discouraged by setbacks, they view them as stepping stones towards greater financial wisdom and success.

Last, Type 7 individuals possess a remarkable focus and discipline when it comes to achieving their financial goals. They have the ability to maintain unwavering focus and commitment, even in the face of distractions and temptations. This discipline allows them to stay motivated and make consistent progress towards their financial objectives. Type 7 individuals understand the importance of setting clear financial goals, creating a roadmap to achieve them, and holding themselves accountable. Their ability to stay disciplined sets them apart and ensures their long-term financial success.

Type 7 individuals possess a range of strengths that, when fully embraced and utilized, can lead to significant financial success. Through their adventurous nature, optimism, adaptability, enthusiasm, multitasking abilities, resilience, creativity, focus, and ability to find joy in abundance, Type 7 individuals have the potential to achieve their financial goals and create a life of financial fulfillment. By recognizing and leveraging these strengths, Type 7 individuals can navigate the complexities of finance with confidence, create innovative financial strategies, and ultimately establish a healthy and prosperous financial future.

Practical Steps for Type 7's Financial

Growth

Now that they have a deeper understanding of the financial mindset and behaviors commonly associated with Type 7 individuals, let's explore some practical steps they can take to foster their financial growth. Type 7s thrive on excitement and new experiences, and they have a desire for freedom and variety, which can influence their approach to finances. However, these traits can also present challenges when it comes to money management. With that in mind, here are some practical strategies for Type 7s to develop a more mindful and successful financial journey.

1. Set Clear Financial Goals and Priorities:

One of the first steps for Type 7s to take is to set clear financial goals and priorities. This involves identifying what they truly want to achieve with their finances and the lifestyle they desire. By honing in on their priorities, Type 7s can direct their financial decisions towards what truly matters to them. Whether it's saving for a dream vacation, starting a business, or building a comfortable retirement fund, having clear goals will serve as a guiding compass on their financial journey.

2. Implement a Budgeting System:

Budgeting is a crucial tool for Type 7s to bring structure and discipline to their financial habits. While it is common for Type 7s to resist constraints, having a budget can actually provide them with a sense of control over their finances and enable them to make informed decisions. By tracking their income, expenses, and savings, Type 7s can ensure that they are aligning their spending with their priorities and maintaining a healthy financial balance.

3. Consider the Long-Term Consequences of Impulsive Spending:

Type 7s are known for their spontaneous and impulsive nature, which can sometimes lead to unwise financial decisions. However, it's important for them to take a step back and consider the long-term consequences of impulsive spending. Before making a purchase, Type 7s can ask themselves if it aligns with their financial goals and if they genuinely need it. By practicing this conscious decision-making process, they can avoid unnecessary expenses and stay on track towards their desired financial outcomes.

4. Embrace Delayed Gratification:

While instant gratification may be tempting, Type 7s can benefit greatly from embracing delayed gratification. This involves saving and investing their money for future experiences and goals. Rather than succumbing to impulsive spending, Type 7s can adopt a mindset of patiently working towards their financial aspirations. By focusing on the long-term rewards, they can channel their excitement towards building a secure and prosperous future.

5. Set Realistic Financial Expectations:

Type 7s often have grand visions and high expectations for their financial endeavors. While having ambitious goals is admirable, it's important for Type 7s to set realistic expectations that align with their current financial situation and resources. By breaking their goals down into smaller, attainable milestones, Type 7s can create a sense of progress and avoid feeling overwhelmed. This will help them maintain motivation and ensure a sense of accomplishment on their financial journey.

6. Balance Excitement and Stability in Financial Planning:

Type 7s crave excitement and variety, but it's essential for them to strike a balance between their desire for new experiences and the need for financial stability. They can achieve this by developing a financial plan that allows for growth and adventure while also establishing a strong foundation. Type 7s can consider investment options that offer both growth potential and stability, ensuring they have a safety net while still exploring thrilling opportunities.

7. Leverage Creativity and Resourcefulness for Financial Success:

Type 7s possess a natural gift for creativity and resourcefulness, and these qualities can be leveraged to drive financial growth. They can think outside the box when it comes to generating income streams or finding innovative ways to save money. Whether it's starting a side business, exploring new ventures, or finding unique strategies to cut expenses, Type 7s can harness their creativity to uncover hidden financial opportunities and thrive in a dynamic financial landscape.

8. Develop Financial Discipline and Consistency:

To ensure long-term financial success, Type 7s must cultivate discipline and consistency in their financial habits. This involves establishing routines for reviewing and managing their finances, tracking expenses, and automating savings. By developing these habits, Type 7s can create a solid financial foundation and build wealth over time, even in the face of distractions and temptations.

9. Seek Support and Accountability:

Type 7s can greatly benefit from seeking support and accountability when it comes to their financial growth. This may involve partnering with a financial advisor who understands their unique needs and can provide guidance, joining financial support groups, or finding a trusted accountability partner who can help them stay on track with their financial goals. Having external support can offer fresh perspectives, provide motivation, and hold them accountable in their financial journey.

10. Practice Gratitude and Contentment in Financial Matters:

Type 7s often find themselves constantly seeking new experiences and material possessions. However, it's important for them to practice gratitude and contentment in their financial lives. By shifting their focus towards appreciating what they already have, Type 7s can cultivate a sense of fulfillment and happiness that extends beyond material possessions. This mindset can help them make more intentional and grounded financial decisions while fostering a healthier relationship with money.

11. Navigating the Fear of Missing Out (FOMO) and Managing Impulsive Spending:

Type 7s are particularly susceptible to the fear of missing out (FOMO), which can lead to impulsive spending. To manage this challenge, Type 7s can implement a 24-hour waiting period for major purchases. This allows them to pause, reflect, and make a more rational decision rather than succumbing to immediate impulses. Practicing mindfulness techniques, such as deep breathing or meditation, can also help Type 7s manage impulsive behaviors and make more conscious choices.

By adopting a mindful approach to financial decision-making, embracing delayed gratification, setting realistic expectations, and leveraging their natural strengths, Type 7s can navigate the complexities of finance with confidence. Additionally, by cultivating discipline, seeking support, practicing gratitude, and managing impulsive tendencies, Type 7s can create a healthy and prosperous financial future while still enjoying the excitement and freedom they crave.

Chapter 9: The Challenger (Type 8)

The Challenger's Money Mindset

At the core of Type 8's money mindset lies their driving motivation for power and control. These individuals have an innate desire to be in charge, to accumulate wealth, and create a sense of security. They thrive on the feeling of being autonomous and self-reliant, as it provides them with a greater sense of power and control over their financial resources. This motivation can be attributed to their need for security, as they believe that financial independence equates to a heightened sense of personal power.

However, beneath the surface, Type 8 individuals grapple with a fear of vulnerability and financial loss. They fear being reliant on others and losing control over their finances. This fear can impact their willingness to take risks, as they often prioritize maintaining their sense of control and security over potential opportunities for growth. Consequently, they tend to adopt an assertive approach to financial decision-making, relying on their self-reliance and determination to navigate the financial landscape.

Furthermore, challengers exhibit a strong inclination towards financial independence and self-sufficiency. They resist relying on others for financial support or partnership, as they perceive it as a potential threat to their autonomy and power. Their innate need for control extends into their financial lives, as they take charge of managing their resources and resist relinquishing control to external entities. This tendency can shape their decision-making, as they prioritize financial freedom and self-sufficiency above all else.

Although Type 8 individuals possess a strong need for control, this can also impact their financial decisions in positive ways. Their desire to be in charge of their financial resources guides them towards making decisions that align with their long-term goals and sense of empowerment. They are adept at creating strategies to cultivate financial stability and security, as they recognize the importance of being in control of their financial destiny.

However, the challenge for Type 8 individuals lies in finding a balance between their desire for control and the benefits of collaboration. They often struggle with recognizing that collaboration and seeking input from others can enhance their financial decision-making. By opening themselves up to the perspectives and expertise of others, they can create more well-rounded financial strategies and forge meaningful partnerships that ultimately support their long-term goals.

To overcome their fear of vulnerability, challengers must embrace healthy risk-taking in their financial decision-making. By striking a balance between assertiveness and openness to new opportunities, they can explore uncharted territories without compromising their sense of personal power. This requires a shift in mindset, where they recognize that vulnerability and risk can lead to growth, rather than being perceived as weaknesses. Taking calculated risks and embracing vulnerability can propel them towards greater financial success and overall empowerment.

Cultivating financial integrity is also crucial for Type 8 individuals. By aligning their financial decisions with their personal values, they create a strong foundation for financial success. Self-reflection and self-awareness play a significant role in this process, as they allow challengers to navigate their decisions with honesty and integrity. By prioritizing financial empowerment alongside their need for control, they can build a financial legacy that is authentic and impactful.

In navigating financial negotiations, Type 8 individuals must manage their assertiveness and temperament. This can be achieved by employing practical strategies such as active listening, empathy, and maintaining an open mind. By understanding the perspectives of others and seeking common ground, they can build successful financial partnerships that benefit all parties involved. Balancing their ambition with empathy is also essential; challengers must consider the impact of their decisions on others, fostering more harmonious and sustainable financial outcomes.

Recognizing the value of collaboration and shared goals is another important aspect of Type 8 individuals' money mindset. By seeking alliances, creating win-win financial scenarios, and focusing on collective success, challengers can enhance their overall financial well-being. They must acknowledge that collaboration does not diminish their power but rather amplifies it on a broader scale.

To summarize, understanding the money mindset of Type 8 individuals requires a deep dive into their motivations, fears, and the impact of their need for control. By recognizing the potential for financial empowerment and integrity, challengers can navigate their financial journeys with greater self-awareness. Embracing vulnerability, healthy risk-taking, collaboration, and empathy are key strategies for Type 8 individuals to achieve financial success while maintaining their sense of personal power.

Financial Struggles and Tendencies of Type 8

Type 8 individuals have an inherent desire for control and independence, which naturally extends to their financial lives. They prefer to be self-reliant and find a sense of empowerment in managing their own finances. This desire for control often leads them to be reluctant to rely on others for financial support, as they fear losing their autonomy and becoming dependent. They are driven to establish financial independence, ensuring that they can make decisions on their own terms without having to answer to anyone.

One of the biggest challenges Type 8s face in their financial journey is their fear of vulnerability. As individuals who seek to maintain a strong and assertive image, they are wary of financial risks that might leave them exposed or in a position of weakness. This fear can manifest in various ways, such as hoarding money to ensure a sense of security or being overly cautious with investments to avoid any potential loss. Type 8s may struggle to trust others with their finances, as they fear being taken advantage of or losing control over their hard-earned resources.

Despite their desire for control, Type 8 individuals can also exhibit impulsive spending habits. This behavior arises from their need to assert their power and autonomy, as well as to demonstrate their ability to indulge in their desires without restraint. Impulsive purchases allow Type 8s to feel a sense of immediate gratification and control over their financial resources. It is important to note that these spending habits may not always align with their long-term financial goals and can lead to financial challenges if left unchecked.

Type 8 individuals' inherent skepticism and reluctance to trust others can create challenges in collaborative financial endeavors. They may find it difficult to enter into joint investments or partnerships, as they fear losing control or being taken advantage of. Type 8s may have an instinctive inclination to make all financial decisions on their own, which can limit their ability to benefit from diverse perspectives and specialized expertise in money management. Learning to cultivate trust and embrace collaboration can open up new opportunities for growth and success.

Type 8 individuals are driven by a strong desire for success and financial dominance. They have an innate need to be at the top, both in terms of status and wealth. This relentless pursuit of financial success can lead them to prioritize accumulating material possessions and amassing personal wealth above all else. While this drive can fuel their motivation and determination in achieving their financial goals, it can also lead to a singular focus on money and an imbalance in other areas of life.

Type 8 individuals face a unique internal conflict when it comes to balancing their desire to be generous and help others with the need to establish and maintain financial boundaries. They may struggle with finding the right balance between being open-hearted and setting limits to protect their own financial well-being. This conflict arises from their strong sense of justice and fairness, as well as their desire to support and empower others. Type 8s must learn to navigate this tension and establish healthy boundaries that allow them to be both generous and financially responsible.

Type 8 individuals may face difficulties when it comes to managing debt and financial responsibilities. Their aversion to feeling controlled or indebted to others can result in an aversion to taking on any form of debt. They may resist borrowing money, even when it could be strategically beneficial, due to the fear of losing control over their financial freedom. This aversion to debt can sometimes hinder their ability to leverage financial opportunities or invest in assets that could potentially yield significant returns.

Type 8 individuals have a tendency to avoid vulnerable emotions, which can significantly influence their financial decision-making. By sidestepping emotional considerations, they may make impulsive or overly aggressive investment decisions. They might prioritize immediate gain over long-term stability or risk-taking over thoughtful analysis.

Recognizing and addressing this tendency is crucial for Type 8s to make more balanced and informed financial choices.

For Type 8 individuals, developing healthy financial relationships is of utmost importance. By cultivating relationships characterized by trust, collaboration, and balanced power dynamics, they can navigate their financial journeys more effectively. Type 8s must learn to leverage their strength and assertiveness towards building partnerships that are mutually beneficial and align with their long-term goals. Valuing the input and expertise of others can provide a broader perspective and enhance their financial decision-making process.

Type 8 individuals can overcome their financial challenges through self-awareness and personal growth. By developing a deeper understanding of their motivations, fears, and individual patterns, they can navigate their financial decisions with greater clarity and purpose. Embracing vulnerability, seeking input from others, and engaging in open and honest dialogue about money can prove transformative for Type 8s as they strive towards financial empowerment and growth.

Despite the challenges they may face, Type 8 individuals possess immense potential for financial empowerment and integrity. By harnessing their strength, passion, and unwavering sense of integrity, they can create a positive impact in their financial lives and the lives of others. Type 8s have the capacity to wield their financial resources in a way that aligns with their values, supports their goals, and empowers those around them. By embracing self-awareness and personal growth, Type 8s can unlock their full potential and make a lasting mark in the realm of money.

Embracing Type 8's Strengths for Financial well-being

Type 8 individuals possess a myriad of strengths that can be harnessed for financial well-being. Their natural self-confidence and assertiveness empower them to take risks and make bold financial decisions. Type 8s have an unwavering belief in their abilities and are unafraid to assert themselves in pursuit of their financial goals. This self-assuredness allows them to navigate the financial landscape with a sense of purpose and determination.

One of the key strengths that Type 8s bring to the table is their direct communication style. They value honesty and transparency, and this extends to their financial dealings as well. Type 8s are willing to address financial issues head-on, whether it's negotiating a contract, discussing investment opportunities, or resolving conflicts related to money. Their straightforward approach contributes to financial integrity and prevents misunderstandings or unethical behavior.

Type 8 individuals excel in decision-making, demonstrating a decisive and direct approach to financial matters. They have a knack for assessing situations quickly, weighing the pros and cons, and taking action. This characteristic makes them effective in financial planning and execution. Type 8s are not afraid to make tough choices when it comes to their finances, allowing them to make sound decisions that lead to long-term success and stability.

The natural leadership skills of Type 8s also play a significant role in their financial empowerment. They have a commanding presence and the ability to inspire others to take control of their financial futures. Type 8s take the lead in financial decision-making, guiding and motivating those around them to embrace financial responsibility and pursue their goals. Their leadership contributes to the empowerment of not only themselves but also their communities.

Resilience and determination are ingrained in the Type 8 personality. In the face of financial challenges and setbacks, Type 8s demonstrate the strength to bounce back and persevere. They refuse to let obstacles define them, using their inherent resilience to overcome financial difficulties. Type 8s are driven by a deep sense of determination that allows them to stay focused and motivated on their financial journey.

While Type 8 individuals have many strengths that contribute to financial well-being, it is important for them to recognize the need for balance and collaboration. Their dominant and assertive nature may sometimes overshadow the value of seeking input from others and considering different perspectives. Type 8s can strive to find a balance between their independence and the benefits of collaborative financial decision-making. By embracing collaboration, they can gain valuable insights and avoid potential blind spots in their financial strategy.

Type 8 individuals possess a unique set of strengths that can be leveraged for financial well-being. Through harnessing their self-confidence, employing direct communication, embracing decision-making skills, cultivating leadership, navigating challenges with resilience, recognizing the need for balance and collaboration, and building healthy financial relationships, Type 8s can achieve financial empowerment and integrity. By utilizing their inherent qualities effectively and embracing personal growth, Type 8 individuals can make a significant impact in the realm of money.

Practical Steps for Type 8's Financial Transformation

1: Understanding the Financial Characteristics of Type 8 Individuals

One significant characteristic of Type 8s is their innate desire for control. they prefer to be in charge of their financial destiny, making independent decisions and taking full responsibility for the outcomes. While this self-assuredness can be advantageous, it can also lead to a reluctance to seek advice or consider alternative perspectives. Recognizing the importance of balance and opening themselves up to differing opinions can help us make more informed financial choices.

Their assertiveness can be a double-edged sword, particularly when it comes to financial negotiations. While their direct and decisive nature can be advantageous in securing favorable deals, it is essential to balance assertiveness with diplomacy. By maintaining clear communication, setting boundaries, and showing respect for the other party's interests, they can achieve mutually beneficial outcomes.

2: Identifying Financial Goals and Aspirations for Type 8 Individuals

To embark on their financial transformation journey, it is crucial for us, as Type 8 individuals, to clearly define their financial goals and aspirations. This process requires us to align their objectives with their strengths and values, ensuring that their pursuit of financial success remains meaningful and fulfilling.

They can start by reflecting on their values and what truly matters to us. What are their long-term aspirations? What legacy do they hope to leave behind? Once they have a clear vision of their desired financial future, they can break it down into specific and measurable goals using the SMART (Specific, Measurable, Achievable, Relevant, and Time-bound) framework.

For instance, instead of having a vague goal of building wealth, they can define it more precisely, such as saving a specific amount for retirement in a given timeframe. By setting concrete goals, they provide themselves with a clear target to work towards, increasing their motivation and focus.

3: Embracing Financial Empowerment and Integrity

One way to empower themselves is by investing in financial education. By acquiring knowledge about personal finance, investing, and other relevant topics, they equip themselves with the tools needed to make informed financial decisions. This can include reading books, attending seminars, or working with financial advisors who can guide us on their journey.

Furthermore, they must approach their financial endeavors with integrity. Engaging in honest and ethical financial practices not only builds trust with others but also nurtures a sense of integrity within themselves. By staying true to their values and conducting their financial affairs with transparency and honesty, they can create a solid foundation for long-term financial well-being.

4: Navigating Negotiations and Financial Conflict

As Type 8 individuals, they excel at asserting themselves in negotiations and addressing financial conflicts head-on. However, it is important to keep in mind that there is a fine line between assertiveness and aggression when it comes to these situations.

To navigate negotiations effectively, they must strike a balance between advocating for their interests and respecting the perspectives of others. This can be achieved by actively listening, seeking common ground, and embracing a win-win mindset. By focusing on mutually beneficial outcomes, they can foster productive conversations and build positive relationships that can lead to financial success.

Furthermore, maintaining financial boundaries is crucial in managing conflicts. they must develop the ability to say no when necessary and enforce boundaries that protect their financial well-being. By communicating their boundaries clearly and assertively, they can avoid being taken advantage of and ensure that their financial interests are prioritized.

5: Harnessing the Power of Networking and Connections

As Type 8 individuals, they possess strong leadership qualities and an innate ability to build networks. These attributes can play a pivotal role in achieving their financial goals by opening doors to new opportunities and enabling us to leverage connections effectively.

To harness the power of networking, they must invest time and effort in expanding their professional relationships. This can involve attending industry events, joining relevant professional organizations, or participating in networking groups. By proactively connecting with like-minded individuals and seeking mutually beneficial relationships, they can tap into a wealth of knowledge, expertise, and potential partnerships that can propel their financial success.

Creating a strong network also provides us with access to valuable opportunities in the realm of finance. Whether it is investment opportunities, potential clients, or industry insights, their network can be a reliable source of information and support. Therefore, it is crucial to cultivate and nurture relationships by offering their expertise, support, and resources to others as well.

6: Balancing Risk and Prudence in Financial Decision-Making

As Type 8 individuals, they are naturally inclined toward risk-taking. This boldness can be advantageous in seizing opportunities and making bold financial moves. However, it is essential to balance their risk appetite with prudence to avoid detrimental consequences.

Before making significant financial decisions, they must conduct thorough research and seek expert advice. By gathering reliable information, analyzing potential risks, and evaluating expected returns, they can make well-informed choices that align with their financial goals.

Diversification is another key aspect of managing risk. By spreading their investments across different asset classes or industries, they can mitigate the impact of any single investment's performance on their overall financial well-being. Diversification allows us to capitalize on the potential for growth while reducing the vulnerability of their portfolio to market fluctuations.

Furthermore, incorporating risk management strategies, such as setting stop-loss levels, regularly reviewing investment performance, and maintaining emergency funds, can provide us with a safety net and protect us from excessive financial risks.

7: Building Financial Resilience and Adaptability

Financial challenges are inevitable, and as Type 8 individuals, they have the strength to persevere through tough times. However, it is essential to actively build financial resilience and adaptability to weather these challenges successfully.

One practical step involves creating an emergency fund. By setting aside a portion of their income for unexpected expenses, they create a financial buffer that reduces stress and allows us to overcome unforeseen circumstances without derailing their long-term goals.

Additionally, diversifying their income sources can enhance their financial resilience. Rather than relying solely on a single income stream, exploring opportunities for additional revenue streams or side businesses can provide us with multiple sources of financial stability and reduce the impact of any one source diminishing or disappearing.

Another crucial aspect of adaptability is staying abreast of industry trends and market changes. The financial landscape is constantly evolving, and they must remain flexible in their investment strategies and financial decisions. Regularly reviewing and adjusting their financial plans can help us adapt to changing circumstances and seize new opportunities.

8: Wealth Creation with a Purpose

While financial success is indeed desirable, as Type 8 individuals, they can go beyond mere accumulation of wealth. It is important for us to align their financial pursuits with a greater purpose and strive to create a meaningful impact in their own lives and the lives of others.

They can do this by identifying causes or organizations that resonate with their values and using their resources to contribute to their success. Whether through philanthropy, impact investing, or financially supporting causes that align with their passions, they can use their financial resources to make a positive difference in the world.

By shifting their focus from personal gain to a larger purpose, they cultivate a sense of fulfillment and satisfaction that goes beyond monetary wealth.

9: Cultivating a Healthy Relationship with Money

It is essential for us to develop a healthy relationship with money. This involves understanding their attitudes and beliefs around money and implementing strategies to ensure that their financial well-being is aligned with their overall well-being.

One practical exercise is to engage in self-reflection about their money mindset. Are they driven purely by financial success, or do they have a healthy balance between personal and financial goals? By understanding their motivations and desires, they can make conscious choices that align with their values and long-term happiness.

Expressing gratitude for what they have and practicing conscious spending are also critical aspects of fostering a healthy relationship with money. Taking the time to appreciate their financial circumstances and the opportunities that money can provide can help us cultivate a sense of contentment and reduce the urge for excessive consumption.

Additionally, by consciously considering their spending habits and focusing on purchases that bring long-term value or align with their values, they can avoid impulsive and wasteful spending.

10: Implementing and Monitoring Financial Plans

Ultimately, an effective financial transformation requires us to put their plans into action and monitor their progress along the way. By implementing a systematic approach to their financial plans, they can ensure that they stay on track and continue to make progress towards their goals.

Implementing their plans involves taking the necessary steps to execute their financial strategies. This can include automating savings, setting up investment accounts, or organizing their financial documentation. By simplifying and streamlining their financial processes, they can reduce friction and increase their commitment to their financial goals.

Monitoring their financial plans ensures that they stay accountable and make adjustments as needed. Regularly reviewing their progress, analyzing the performance of their investments, and staying informed about changes in the financial landscape allow us to adapt and make necessary modifications to their plans to drive continued financial success.

Type 8 individuals, they possess unique strengths that, when harnessed effectively, can lead to significant financial transformation. By recognizing the financial characteristics that shape their behavior, setting clear goals, embracing financial empowerment and integrity, navigating negotiations and conflicts, harnessing the power of networking, balancing risk and prudence, building resilience and adaptability, aligning their pursuit of wealth with a greater purpose, cultivating a healthy relationship with money, and implementing and monitoring their financial plans, they can achieve financial empowerment and integrity. Let us embrace their strengths, remain determined, and continue on this journey towards financial well-being.

Chapter 10: The Peacemaker (Type 9)

The Peacemaker's Money Mentality

As a Type 9 individual, I have been intimately acquainted with the peacemaker's money mentality. The way they view money and the decisions they make around it are heavily influenced by our core motivations, fears, and desires. In this chapter, we delve into the mindset of a peacemaker when it comes to finances, and explore how they can shift their perspective to cultivate abundance.

For a Type 9, financial decisions are driven by a deep desire for harmony and peace. They strive to create a balanced and conflict-free environment in all aspects of their lives, including money. This often leads them to avoid confrontational or contentious financial situations, as they disrupt the harmony they crave. Consequently, they may find themselves overlooking their own financial needs and sacrificing their own well-being to maintain peace in our relationships.

One of the challenges they face is the fear of conflict. This fear can manifest in various ways when it comes to money. They may avoid discussions about finances, suppress our own desires and goals, or even merge our financial concerns with others to keep the peace. This fear hinders our ability to assert our financial needs and take initiative in pursuing our own financial growth.

Another aspect of the peacemaker's money mentality is our aversion to stress. Type 9 individuals tend to seek stability and security, and financial stress is seen as a threat to the peace they crave. they may avoid taking risks or making bold financial decisions for fear of disrupting the equilibrium in our lives. While this mentality may provide temporary relief, it can also limit our financial opportunities and hinder our journey towards abundance.

To overcome these challenges, it is essential for Type 9 individuals to cultivate self-awareness and embrace a mindset of abundance. This begins with acknowledging our tendency to prioritize the needs of others over our own and recognizing the importance of setting healthy financial boundaries. By nurturing a balanced sense of harmony within ourselves, they can create a solid foundation for our financial well-being.

Taking ownership of our financial decisions and setting meaningful goals is also key to embracing abundance. They must learn to overcome our natural inclination towards procrastination and develop strategies that enable us to take action and move forward. Integrating qualities from Type 3 and Type 6, such as ambition and planning, can support our financial growth and empowerment.

Visualization techniques can be powerful tools for Type 9 individuals on their journey to abundance. By envisioning themselves in a state of financial well-being, they can activate their subconscious mind and manifest their desires. This practice helps to shift their perspective from scarcity to abundance and enables us to attract opportunities and resources that align with their financial goals.

While it is important to nurture our own financial well-being, they must also recognize the value of seeking support from financial professionals and mentors. Their expertise can enhance our financial knowledge and decision-making skills, empowering us to make informed choices and create a solid financial foundation.

As a Type 9 individual, our money mentality is heavily influenced by our strong desire for harmony and our aversion to conflict and stress. However, by embracing a mindset of abundance and cultivating self-awareness, they can overcome our natural inclinations and create a healthy relationship with money. By setting clear financial boundaries, taking ownership of our decisions, and seeking support, they can unlock our full potential for financial growth and create a life of peace and abundance.

Financial Challenges Faced by Type 9

As a Type 9 individual, I have come to understand the unique financial challenges that accompany my personality type. My tendency to avoid conflict and prioritize peace and tranquility often impacts my approach to money. Instead of actively engaging with financial matters, I find myself more drawn to creating a harmonious and peaceful environment. While this desire for harmony is admirable, it can sometimes hinder my ability to effectively manage my finances.

One of the biggest challenges I face is indecisiveness when it comes to making financial decisions. I tend to procrastinate and avoid taking action, as I fear making the wrong choice and disrupting the peace. This indecisiveness can be paralyzing, preventing me from moving forward and taking the necessary steps to secure my financial future.

Setting clear financial goals is another area where I struggle as a Type 9 individual. My desire for peace and avoidance of conflict can hinder me from taking proactive steps towards financial advancement. It is challenging for me to clearly define my financial objectives and develop a plan to achieve them, as I often prioritize maintaining harmony over assertively pursuing financial initiatives.

Moreover, my natural inclination towards avoiding confrontation and my preference for maintaining harmony often result in a lack of assertiveness when it comes to financial matters. I find it difficult to assert myself in financial situations, whether it is negotiating a contract or advocating for fair compensation. My aversion to conflict can sometimes lead to settling for less than what I deserve or missing out on financial opportunities.

Another challenge I face is the tendency to overspend and become financially complacent. Rather than addressing financial issues directly, I often avoid them, leading to overspending as a way to temporarily alleviate any discomfort or stress. This complacency can prevent me from taking proactive steps to improve my financial situation and create long-term financial stability.

Additionally, as a Type 9 individual, I have a strong aversion to financial conflicts and disagreements. I tend to avoid addressing these conflicts directly, which can have severe consequences on my financial well-being. By avoiding necessary conversations and actions, I risk allowing unresolved financial issues to accumulate and negatively impact my financial stability.

I also have a natural inclination to merge my finances with others, such as a partner. While this can foster a sense of unity and harmony, it may also create challenges and implications for my individual financial growth and decision-making. It is important for me to maintain a balance between merging finances and maintaining personal financial independence.

Furthermore, I tend to prioritize the needs of others over my own financial well-being. This lack of self-advocacy can have long-term consequences for my financial stability and security. It is crucial for me to recognize the importance of prioritizing my own financial needs and taking proactive steps to ensure my financial well-being.

Another significant challenge for me is the difficulty in advocating for myself in financial transactions. I often struggle to assert my needs or negotiate effectively, which can result in me accepting less favorable terms or missing out on financial opportunities. Developing assertiveness and self-advocacy skills in financial matters is essential for overcoming this challenge.

Over-reliance on others for financial decision making is another obstacle that I face as a Type 9 individual. I tend to rely on others for guidance and decision making, which can inhibit my ability to develop independent financial skills and knowledge. It is crucial for me to take ownership of my financial decisions and actively participate in the decision-making process.

In order to overcome these unique financial challenges, I have found several strategies to be helpful. First and foremost, cultivating a mindset of abundance is vital. By acknowledging and addressing my tendencies to prioritize the needs of others and set healthy boundaries, I can create a solid foundation for my financial well-being.

Taking ownership of my financial decisions and setting meaningful goals is also crucial. Overcoming my natural inclination towards procrastination and taking action is essential for financial growth and empowerment. Integrating qualities from Type 3 and Type 6, such as ambition and planning, can support my journey towards financial abundance.

Utilizing visualization techniques can be a powerful tool for me. By visualizing myself in a state of financial well-being, I can activate my subconscious mind and manifest my desires. This practice helps shift my perspective from scarcity to abundance and enables me to attract opportunities and resources that align with my financial goals.

While nurturing my own financial well-being, seeking support from financial professionals and mentors is also essential. Their expertise can enhance my financial knowledge and decision-making skills, empowering me to make informed choices and create a solid financial foundation.

As a Type 9 individual, my money mentality is heavily influenced by my strong desire for harmony and aversion to conflict and stress. However, by embracing a mindset of abundance and cultivating self-awareness, I can overcome my natural inclinations and create a healthy relationship with money. By setting clear financial boundaries, taking ownership of my decisions, and seeking support, I can unlock my full potential for financial growth and create a life of peace and abundance.

Utilizing Type 9's Strengths for Financial Success

As a Type 9 individual, I have discovered that my natural strengths and characteristics can be leveraged to achieve financial success and stability. By embracing these strengths and taking proactive steps, I am able to navigate the world of money with confidence and create a foundation of lasting financial well-being.

One of the key strengths of Type 9 individuals is their ability to maintain a sense of inner peace and balance. This peace-seeking nature can be extremely advantageous when it comes to managing finances. I have found that by prioritizing a balanced budget, I am able to create a sense of peace and security in my financial life. By ensuring that my income aligns with my expenses and saving a portion of my earnings, I am able to maintain stability and avoid unnecessary stress or worry about my financial situation.

Type 9 individuals also have a natural inclination to go with the flow and adapt to various situations. This adaptability can be a valuable asset when it comes to identifying and embracing passive income opportunities. Whether it be through investments or rental properties, I have learned to harness my ability to embrace change and seize opportunities that can generate additional income. By diversifying my income streams and embracing passive income, I am able to create a sense of financial security and freedom.

Another strength that I have discovered is my ability to navigate conflicts and negotiations with ease. While I may have a natural aversion to conflict, I have learned to harness this tendency and utilize it as a negotiation tool. By approaching negotiations with a calm and composed demeanor, I am able to achieve better financial outcomes, such as negotiating higher salary offers or securing favorable business deals. My conflict-avoidant nature allows me to remain level-headed and find mutually beneficial solutions that create win-win situations.

In addition to my conflict-avoidant nature, my desire for harmony and avoiding conflicts also contributes to healthy financial dynamics in my relationships. By prioritizing open communication, shared financial goals, and mutual respect, I am able to cultivate financial harmony in my relationships. This not only fosters a sense of unity and teamwork but also ensures that financial decisions are made with the overall well-being of both parties in mind.

As a Type 9 individual, I have a natural gift for creativity and the ability to see multiple perspectives. I have leveraged these qualities to explore new and unconventional ways of generating income and expanding my financial opportunities. By thinking outside of the box and being open to new ideas, I have been able to tap into my creative potential and uncover innovative methods of financial growth. Whether it be starting a side business or pursuing a passion project, I have found that harnessing my creativity allows me to bring in additional income while also fulfilling my personal interests and values.

However, as a Type 9 individual, I am not immune to the challenges that can arise in managing finances. One obstacle that I frequently face is the tendency to procrastinate in financial matters. I have learned to overcome this challenge by setting clear goals, creating routines, and seeking external accountability. By breaking down financial tasks into manageable steps and establishing a consistent routine, I am able to tackle them head-on and avoid the pitfalls of procrastination.

Another important step that I have taken to improve my financial situation is seeking support and accountability. By working with a financial advisor or joining a financial accountability group, I am able to receive guidance, feedback, and support on my financial journey. These individuals provide me with invaluable insights and hold me accountable to my goals, pushing me to take action and make informed financial decisions.

Mindfulness has also played a significant role in my journey towards financial success. By practicing mindfulness, I am able to make deliberate and conscious financial decisions, avoiding impulsive choices that may have negative long-term consequences. Mindfulness allows me to be fully present and aware of my financial actions, ensuring that each decision aligns with my values and long-term financial stability.

Creating a vision for my financial future has been instrumental in guiding my financial decisions and actions. By envisioning my ideal financial life, I am able to align my financial goals with my values and desires. This vision serves as a guiding light, motivating me to take the necessary steps to manifest my financial dreams. Through goal setting and action planning, I am able to bring my vision to life and create the financial future I desire.

Navigating financial conflicts and asserting my needs is an ongoing challenge for me as a Type 9 individual. However, I have learned to communicate effectively, set personal boundaries, and find a balance between maintaining harmony and advocating for my own financial well-being. By practicing effective communication and setting clear boundaries, I am able to address financial conflicts in a respectful and assertive manner, ensuring that my needs are met without compromising the overall goal of harmony.

Embracing financial stability is paramount to my financial success as a Type 9 individual. By prioritizing saving, investing wisely, and minimizing financial stress, I am able to create a solid foundation of financial stability. Financial stability allows me to cultivate peace in my life and frees me from the constant worry and stress that can arise from financial instability.

While financial responsibilities are important, I have also learned to strike a balance between my financial obligations and self-care. By prioritizing my own well-being and finding a balance between work and personal life, I am able to ensure long-term financial success and overall satisfaction. This balance allows me to thrive in all areas of life, not just financially, fostering a sense of abundance and fulfillment.

As a Type 9 individual, I have discovered that my natural strengths and characteristics can be harnessed to achieve financial success and stability. By embracing my peace-seeking nature, adaptability, conflict-avoidant tendencies, desire for harmony, and creativity, I am able to navigate the world of money with confidence and create a solid foundation for my financial well-being. By overcoming challenges such as procrastination, seeking support and accountability, practicing mindfulness, creating a financial vision, and embracing financial stability, I am able to integrate these strengths into my daily financial practices for long-lasting success and fulfillment. Through proactive steps and a commitment to personal growth, I can unlock my full potential and create a life of peace and abundance in all areas, including my finances.

Practical Strategies for Type 9's Financial

Growth

1. Embrace your peace-seeking nature: Use your ability to remain level-headed and find mutually beneficial solutions to negotiate and make financial decisions that maintain harmony and peace in your life and relationships.

2. Prioritize open communication: Create an environment of open communication with your partner or family members when it comes to finances. By discussing shared financial goals, desires, and concerns, you can ensure that financial decisions are made with the overall well-being of everyone involved.

3. Tap into your creativity: Leverage your natural gift for creativity to explore new and unconventional ways of generating income and expanding your financial opportunities. Think outside of the box and be open to new ideas that will not only bring in additional income but also fulfill your personal interests and values.

4. Overcome procrastination: Set clear financial goals, break down tasks into manageable steps, and establish a consistent routine to avoid procrastination and stay on track with your financial responsibilities. Seek external accountability through a financial advisor or an accountability group to keep you motivated and on task.

5. Practice mindfulness: Incorporate mindfulness into your financial decision-making process. By being fully present and aware of your financial actions, you can make deliberate and conscious choices that align with your values and long-term financial stability.

6. Create a vision for your financial future: Envision your ideal financial life and use it as motivation to align your financial goals with your values and desires. By setting specific and achievable financial goals and creating action plans, you can bring your vision to life and create the financial future you desire.

7. Communicate assertively: While maintaining harmony is important to you, it's also crucial to assert your own needs and advocate for your financial well-being. Practice effective communication and set clear boundaries to address financial conflicts in a respectful and assertive manner.

8. Prioritize financial stability: Establish a solid foundation of financial stability by prioritizing saving, investing wisely, and minimizing financial stress. This will allow you to cultivate peace in your life and free yourself from the constant worry and stress that can arise from financial instability.

9. Strike a balance between financial obligations and self-care: Find a balance between your financial responsibilities and self-care. Prioritize your own well-being and self-care practices to ensure long-term financial success and overall satisfaction.

By implementing these practical strategies, Type 9 individuals can unlock their full financial potential and create a life of peace, abundance, and fulfillment in all areas, including their finances.

Chapter 11: The Effect of Wings

Understanding the Concept of Wings

As we delve deeper into the Enneagram system, it becomes evident that the concept of wings plays a pivotal role in shaping our personality and behavior. Similarly, our financial attitudes and approaches are significantly influenced by the interplay of our dominant Enneagram type and its wings. Understanding this connection can offer profound insights into the complexities of our relationship with money.

Within the Enneagram context, wings are often described as the adjacent types that surround our dominant type on the Enneagram diagram. These adjacent types serve as sources of additional traits and characteristics, adding depth and nuance to our overall personality profile. Just as a bird uses its wings to maneuver and navigate its environment, our wings contribute to our emotional and behavioral repertoire, including our financial mindset.

The impact of wings on our personality is multifaceted. They shape our strengths, weaknesses, and motivations, providing a lens through which they view the world and make decisions. Each wing brings forth its unique set of traits, influencing our approach to financial matters. For example, someone with a dominant Type Eight personality may possess strong assertiveness and a desire for control, but their presence of a Type Nine wing could temper their intensity, resulting in a more relaxed and collaborative approach to money.

It is essential to recognize that the presence of a wing modifies and adds nuanced characteristics to an individual's dominant Enneagram type. This interplay can profoundly affect our financial mindset and behaviors. For instance, a Type Three personality with a Type Two wing may exhibit a strong drive for success and achievement, combined with a people-oriented approach to financial interactions. These individuals may excel in sales or entrepreneurship, leveraging their charisma and charm to build relationships and secure financial opportunities.

Understanding our wings is crucial for personal growth and development, not only in the realm of finance but also in all aspects of life. By recognizing the interplay between our dominant type and its wings, they gain a more comprehensive understanding of ourselves and our motivations. This self-awareness allows us to leverage our strengths and address our weaknesses, fostering a healthier relationship with money.

However, it is important to note that the interaction between an individual's dominant Enneagram type and their wings can sometimes create conflicts or synergies concerning financial attitudes. Conflicts may arise when the traits of the wings contradict or clash with the core motivations of the dominant type. For example, a Type Six personality with a Five wing may experience tension between their need for security and their inclination to conserve resources. Conversely, synergies occur when the traits of the wings align with and enhance the primary motivations of the dominant type. An example of this could be a Type One personality with a Type Nine wing, where the wing's desire for peace and harmony meshes well with the One's pursuit of perfection and moral rectitude.

To provide a clearer picture of the diverse manifestations of different combinations of Enneagram types and wings, let's look at two examples. A Type Four personality with a Three wing may exhibit a blend of introspection, creativity, and a drive for recognition and success. In terms of finances, this individual may strive to express their unique identity through their financial choices while also seeking external validation and acknowledgment of their achievements. On the other hand, a Type Seven personality with an Eight wing may combine their sense of adventure and enthusiasm with a bold and assertive approach to money. Such individuals may be drawn to risk-taking opportunities and enjoy the thrill of financial ventures.

It is essential to dispel any misconceptions or oversimplifications associated with the concept of wings. The interaction between an individual's dominant type and their wings is complex and unique to each person. It cannot be reduced to mere stereotypes or predetermined traits. Each individual's journey of self-discovery necessitates an exploration of their dominant type, its wings, and the intricate interplay between the two.

To embark on this journey of self-reflection and self-awareness, practical tips and exercises can be helpful. Journaling, introspection, and engaging in discussions with trusted individuals skilled in the Enneagram system can aid in uncovering and understanding the influence of wings on our financial attitudes. By examining our past financial decisions, motivations, and patterns, they can begin to unravel the underlying dynamics at play.

By acknowledging and embracing the impact of wings on our personality and financial mindset, they open ourselves up to a more holistic understanding of ourselves. This understanding sets the stage for personal and financial transformation. As they continue our exploration of the Enneagram and its relationship with money, they will delve deeper into specific ways in which wings can impact our financial attitudes and behaviors.

In the upcoming chapters, they will explore topics such as how different wing combinations influence risk tolerance, financial goal-setting, and our views on wealth and abundance. By examining these areas, they can find a more precise roadmap for navigating the complex landscape of money and achieving financial well-being.

Wings are an integral part of the Enneagram system, providing depth and complexity to our understanding of personality and its impact on our financial attitudes. By recognizing and exploring our dominant type and its wings, they can gain a profound insight into the forces that shape our financial mindset and behaviors. This journey of self-awareness opens doors to personal growth and transformation, enabling us to build a healthier and more fulfilling relationship with money.

The Influence of Wings on Financial Behaviors

As they delve deeper into the influence of wings on financial behaviors within the Enneagram system, they begin to uncover the profound impact these adjacent types can have on our financial mindset and decision-making. Wings are the complementary types that flank our primary type, influencing and shaping our attitudes and behaviors in various domains, including the realm of finance. Understanding the significance of wings can provide valuable insights into our financial patterns and offer a roadmap for personal and financial growth.

Within the Enneagram system, wings are categorized into stress and security wings. Stress wings represent the adjacent type that influences our behavior when they are under pressure or feeling stressed. On the other hand, security wings refer to the adjacent type that provides a sense of stability and security. These wings play a crucial role in shaping our financial mindset by either amplifying or mitigating the inherent traits and tendencies of our primary type.

Individuals with stress wings often exhibit specific financial behaviors when facing pressure or stress. For example, a Type One personality with a Nine wing may become more risk-averse and conservative with their financial decisions when feeling overwhelmed. They may prioritize stability or preserving resources over potential opportunities for growth. Conversely, a Type Eight personality with a Seven wing may be more driven to take risks and seek exciting financial ventures when under stress, embracing the adrenaline rush of high-stakes investments. By exploring how stress wings impact our risk tolerance, financial goals, and attitudes towards money, they gain a deeper understanding of our financial patterns and challenges.

In contrast, individuals with security wings tend to exhibit more stable financial behaviors and decision-making. A Type Six personality with a Five wing may emphasize long-term financial planning, prioritizing economic security and the accumulation of knowledge and resources. They may be more cautious and methodical in their financial strategies, avoiding unnecessary risks. Similarly, a Type Three personality with a Two wing may focus on financial stability by seeking opportunities for collaboration and leveraging their network to achieve their financial goals. These individuals may excel at creating and maintaining prosperous relationships that contribute to their financial success.

It's important to recognize that conflicts can arise when our dominant type and wings have contrasting tendencies or motivations. These internal tensions can create inconsistent or conflicting financial behaviors. Understanding and navigating these conflicts is key to finding balance and alignment within our financial decisions. By acknowledging the potential clashes between our core type and wings, they can develop strategies to address and integrate these differences, ultimately creating a more harmonious approach to money.

Awareness of our wing influences can significantly enhance our financial growth and fulfillment. By embracing the strengths and perspectives of our wings, they can leverage their positive attributes and mitigate challenges. This self-awareness allows us to make more informed financial decisions that align with our core motivations and values. Practical exercises and advice can help us harness the positive aspects of our wings, whether it's exploring our risk tolerance, setting financial goals, or developing healthy attitudes towards money.

Just as our primary type and wings can evolve and grow over time, so too can our financial attitudes and behaviors. It's crucial to continuously reflect on and reassess our wing influences to adapt our financial mindset and actions accordingly. By remaining open to self-reflection and self-awareness, they can ensure that our financial decisions align with our ever-changing needs and aspirations. Tracking and reassessing our wing influences through tools and techniques allows us to stay in tune with our evolving selves and stay on the path of financial wellbeing.

The interaction between our core type, wings, and other factors such as instinctual variants and subtypes further adds complexity to our financial behaviors and outlook. Exploring these intersections deepens our understanding of how these various influences interact and shape our financial choices. Real-life examples and case studies can illuminate these complexities, providing a rich tapestry of personal experiences that highlight the unique interplay between our dominant type, wings, and other influencing factors.

Although the influence of wings on our financial behaviors can bring immense growth and understanding, it is not without its challenges. Misconceptions and myths associated with wings can hinder our progress, leading to misunderstandings or oversimplifications. Overcoming these challenges requires a commitment to embracing the nuances and complexities of our dominant type and wings. By dispelling these misconceptions and offering guidance for navigating potential pitfalls, they can align our financial actions with our core type and wings, fostering a more authentic and purposeful relationship with money.

Integrating our core type and wing influences is the key to a holistic and balanced approach to money. By embracing the strengths and perspectives that our wings offer, they can create a comprehensive understanding of our financial mindset and behaviors. This integration allows us to leverage the strengths of our wings, harmonize conflicting tendencies, and ultimately guide us towards a more fulfilling and meaningful financial journey. With a deep understanding of the influence of wings on our financial behaviors and an intentional embrace of their impact, they can cultivate a healthier and more prosperous relationship with money.

Leveraging the Strengths of Wings for Financial Success

As they delve deeper into the exploration of the Enneagram and its relationship with money, it becomes clear that understanding and leveraging the strengths of our wings is essential for financial success. The concept of wings in the Enneagram system refers to the two adjacent personality types that influence and complement our dominant type. These wings contribute nuances, strengths, and perspectives to our core personality, shaping our behaviors and mindset in various aspects of life, including finances.

Recognizing the significance of wings in our financial behaviors and mindset allows us to utilize their positive qualities for abundance and fulfillment. Each wing brings unique perspectives and traits that can have a profound impact on our financial journey. Let's begin by examining the Perfectionist wing of Type 1, a meticulous and conscientious personality. Individuals with a Type 1 core who possess a Perfectionist wing can leverage their attention to detail, discipline, and integrity to excel in financial matters. These individuals are likely to be diligent savers, careful with their spending, and have a strong sense of financial responsibility. Their adherence to high standards and their commitment to doing things right can contribute to their financial success and establish a solid foundation for wealth accumulation.

Moving on to Type 2 individuals, they encounter the Helper wing. Type 2 personalities are naturally giving, compassionate, and empathetic. When they embrace the strengths of their Helper wing, they can utilize these qualities to foster financial abundance and fulfillment. Sensitive to the needs and desires of others, Type 2s with a strong Helper wing can excel in fields where their people skills are valued, such as sales and client relations. By channeling their natural inclination to support and uplift others, they can build strong networks and establish connections that contribute to their financial growth. Furthermore, their empathy and understanding can lead them to opportunities where they can provide valuable solutions, resulting in financial rewards and personal fulfillment.

Next, they turn our attention to the Achiever wing of Type 3 personalities. Type 3 individuals are driven, ambitious, and focused on achievement and success. When they embrace the strengths of their Achiever wing, they become unstoppable forces in pursuing financial goals. Type 3s with a dominant Achiever wing are goal-oriented and capable of implementing efficient strategies to achieve financial success. Their natural inclination for productivity and their desire for recognition motivate them to excel in their chosen fields, often leading to professional and financial advancement. Their determination and ability to adapt to changing circumstances enable them to stay ahead in the competitive world of finance.

Type 4 personalities, known as Individualists, possess a depth of emotional intelligence and creativity. When they tap into the strengths of their Individualist wing, their financial stability and creative pursuits are enhanced. Type 4s with a strong Individualist wing approach money and finances from a unique perspective. They value authenticity and seek financial endeavors that align with their personal values and creative pursuits. Their passion for self-expression can lead them towards unconventional financial paths, such as entrepreneurship or artistic ventures, where they can channel their creativity and find financial stability. By embracing their individuality and integrating it into their financial decisions, Type 4s can find fulfillment and success in both their artistic endeavors and their financial pursuits.

Moving on to Type 5, the Investigator personality, they encounter their Investigator wing. Type 5 individuals exhibit traits such as curiosity, introspection, and a thirst for knowledge. When they harness the strengths of their Investigator wing, they can utilize their natural inclination for strategic thinking and analysis to achieve financial security and make wise investments. Type 5s with a prominent Investigator wing may excel in fields that require in-depth research and expertise, such as financial planning or investment analysis. Their disciplined approach to gathering information and their inherently calculated mindset enable them to make informed financial decisions with a focus on long-term security and growth.

Type 6 personalities, known as Loyalists, possess a strong sense of loyalty, commitment, and risk awareness. When they embrace the strengths of their Loyalist wing, they become experts in cultivating financial confidence and managing risk. Type 6s with a dominant Loyalist wing may approach financial decisions with caution and thorough analysis, avoiding unnecessary risks and seeking stability. Their loyalty to trusted financial advisors or institutions can lead to long-term financial success, as they consistently make informed and calculated decisions. In an ever-changing financial landscape, their risk management skills and commitment to financial security provide them with a solid foundation for flourishing in their financial endeavors.

The Enthusiast wing of Type 7 personalities brings a sense of excitement, innovation, and adaptability to their financial journey. Type 7 individuals naturally seek variety, stimulation, and new opportunities. By incorporating the strengths of their Enthusiast wing, they can drive financial success through innovative and adaptive approaches. Type 7s with a strong Enthusiast wing are unafraid of trying new strategies or seizing opportunities as they arise. Their optimism and ability to pivot enable them to navigate changing market conditions and capitalize on emerging trends. By embracing their adventurous spirit and maintaining an openness to new possibilities, Type 7s can achieve financial growth while enjoying the thrill of the journey.

Type 8, the Challenger, possesses qualities of assertiveness, potheyr, and self-confidence. When they tap into the strengths of their Challenger wing, they experience financial empowerment and assertiveness. Type 8s with a dominant Challenger wing approach their financial endeavors with a strong sense of self-assuredness and determination. Their assertiveness allows them to negotiate favorable terms and conditions, and their desire for control and independence drives them to succeed financially. The ability to assert themselves in financial transactions, assert their worth in negotiations, and assert their influence in their chosen field positions them for financial success and personal fulfillment.

Last, they explore the Peacemaker wing of Type 9 personalities. Type 9 individuals value harmony, peace, and collaboration. When they embrace the strengths of their Peacemaker wing, they promote financial harmony and collaboration. Type 9s with a dominant Peacemaker wing possess a natural ability to foster cooperation and create win-win financial scenarios. Their inclusive mindset and diplomatic approach enable them to navigate financial relationships with ease. By seeking collaborative opportunities and focusing on financial decisions that consider the needs and goals of all parties involved, they promote a harmonious approach to money that benefits not only themselves but also those around them.

As they've seen, each personality type has wings that bring unique perspectives, strengths, and qualities to their financial journey. Integrating and balancing the characteristics of our primary type and wings is crucial for optimal financial success. By recognizing and harnessing the positive influences of our wings, they can align our financial decisions with our core motivations and values. Practical tips and real-life success stories further illuminate how individuals have effectively leveraged their wing strengths for financial fulfillment.

However, it's important to acknowledge that integrating our core type and wing influences is not without challenges. Conflicts and tensions may arise when our dominant type and wings have contrasting tendencies or motivations. Understanding and navigating these conflicts is key to finding balance and alignment within our financial decisions. By acknowledging and addressing potential clashes between our core type and wings, they can develop strategies to integrate and harmonize these differences, ultimately creating a more balanced and purposeful approach to money.

Leveraging the strengths of our wings is fundamental for financial success and fulfillment. By embracing the unique qualities and perspectives of our wings, they can create a comprehensive understanding of our financial mindset and behaviors. This integration allows us to leverage the inherent strengths of our wings, harmonize conflicting tendencies, and guide us towards a more fulfilling and meaningful financial journey. With a deep understanding of the influence of wings on our financial behaviors and an intentional embrace of their impact, they can cultivate a healthier and more prosperous relationship with money.

Balancing the Influence of Wings for Financial well-being

In the intricate world of the Enneagram, our wings play a significant role in shaping our personalities and influencing our behaviors. They provide unique perspectives and amplify certain characteristics of our core type, bringing forth new dimensions to our financial decision-making process. Understanding and harnessing the influence of our wings is essential for achieving financial well-being. In this chapter, they will delve deeper into the concept of wings and explore strategies to maintain a balanced approach to financial decision-making while embracing the strengths of our wings. By doing so, they can unlock our true potential and create a harmonious relationship with money that aligns with our core motivations and values.

Just as birds rely on their wings for flight, they too rely on our wings to navigate the financial landscape. Our wings shape our attitudes towards money and influence the way they make financial decisions. Each wing brings its own distinctive flavor to our financial behaviors, highlighting different aspects of our core type. For example, a Type 1 with a dominant Perfectionist wing may exhibit meticulousness and attention to detail in their financial planning, while a Type 1 with a dominant Achiever wing may focus more on setting ambitious financial goals and striving for success. It is important to recognize that our wings can either enhance or hinder our financial well-being, depending on how they integrate and balance their influences.

To achieve financial success and fulfillment, they must harness the strengths that our wings offer. Each wing brings unique qualities that, when embraced, can propel us forward on our financial journey. For instance, those with a dominant Achiever wing can use their goal-oriented nature and productivity to excel in their chosen fields, leading to professional advancement and financial rewards. Similarly, individuals with a strong Individualist wing can harness their creativity and values to find financial stability in unconventional paths that align with their passions. By embracing and leveraging the strengths of our wings, they can enhance our financial decision-making, find fulfillment, and achieve the success they desire.

While our wings provide strengths, they can also present challenges and pitfalls in our financial decision-making. For example, an Achiever wing may drive someone to prioritize external recognition and success at the expense of their well-being, leading to burnout or overworking. Similarly, an Individualist wing may deter someone from taking practical financial steps due to a strong inclination towards following their creative pursuits. It is crucial to recognize and address these challenges to ensure a healthy and balanced relationship with money. By leveraging strategies such as self-reflection, mindfulness, and seeking guidance from financial professionals, they can navigate the hurdles posed by our wings and find equilibrium in our financial decisions.

Achieving balance between the influence of our wings and other factors in our financial decisions is crucial. While our wings provide valuable insights and strengths, they should not dominate or overshadow other considerations. Integrating the wisdom of our wings with sound financial strategies and long-term goals can lead us to make well-informed decisions that support our overall well-being. By striking a harmonious balance between our wings, our core type, and other elements of our financial lives, they can cultivate a comprehensive and holistic approach to money that promotes growth and fulfillment.

Self-awareness and mindfulness are vital tools in understanding and managing the influence of our wings on financial decisions. By developing an introspective mindset and staying attuned to our motivations, values, and behaviors, they can navigate the complex interplay between our wings and money. Engaging in practices such as meditation, journaling, and regular self-reflection can help us cultivate the necessary self-awareness and mindfulness to make conscious financial choices that align with our core selves and bring fulfillment.

Creating a supportive financial environment that aligns with our wings and values is essential for maintaining a healthy relationship with money. Establishing financial systems and structures that promote a balanced approach can help us stay on track and make financial decisions that support our overall well-being. Additionally, surrounding ourselves with a supportive community and seeking guidance from financial professionals who understand the influence of wings can further enhance our financial journey. By nourishing our financial environment, they create the space for our wings to flourish and contribute to our financial well-being.

Balancing the influence of wings is the key to achieving financial well-being. By recognizing and embracing the strengths of our wings, navigating the challenges they present, and integrating their wisdom into our financial decisions, they can create a harmonious and purposeful relationship with money. Take the time to reflect on your own relationship with money and how your wings may influence your financial decisions. Armed with the strategies and tips provided in this chapter, empower yourself to take action and implement them in your financial life, unlocking your true potential and creating a fulfilling and prosperous financial journey.

Chapter 12: Other Things to Know

Enneagram Compatibility in Financial Partnerships

In the vast world of finance, it is not uncommon for individuals to form partnerships to achieve their financial goals. However, what often goes unnoticed is the impact of Enneagram compatibility in these alliances. The Enneagram, a profound personality framework, offers invaluable insight into the different motivations, fears, and behaviors of individuals. When applied to financial partnerships, understanding the compatibility between Enneagram types becomes crucial for fostering effective collaboration and achieving financial success.

To truly thrive in financial partnerships, it is imperative to recognize and appreciate the distinctive qualities of each Enneagram type. By doing so, they gain a deeper understanding of our partners' perspectives, needs, and strengths, enabling us to navigate potential challenges and find common ground for growth and prosperity. This segment of the book aims to shed light on the intricate dynamics of Enneagram compatibility in financial partnerships, providing practical guidance on how to build harmonious and fruitful collaborations across the nine Enneagram types.

When engaging in financial partnerships with individuals of Type 1, commonly known as the Perfectionists, they encounter individuals driven by a deep sense of moral responsibility and an unwavering desire for perfection. These individuals often exhibit a meticulous approach to financial matters, meticulously analyzing every detail before making decisions. Their dedication to high standards and excellence can be invaluable for avoiding financial pitfalls and ensuring accuracy in financial management.

However, the Perfectionists' relentless pursuit of flawlessness can manifest as an inclination towards pessimism and an aversion to risks. They may have difficulty embracing unconventional approaches or adjusting their plans when circumstances change. To effectively collaborate with Perfectionists, it is essential to acknowledge their need for meticulousness and build trust through open communication. Encouraging them to consider alternative perspectives and allowing room for flexibility can help foster a healthy balance between prudence and adaptability in financial decision-making.

Type 2, known as the Helpers, bring their selfless and nurturing nature into financial partnerships. These individuals have a natural inclination towards caring for others, often extending their generosity and support to their financial endeavors. Type 2 individuals are particularly proficient in cultivating strong relationships, which can be incredibly valuable when it comes to networking, attracting clients, and exploring new opportunities.

However, the Helpers may struggle with setting boundaries and prioritizing their own financial needs. Their tendency to prioritize the needs of others can result in neglecting their financial well-being. To establish mutually beneficial financial partnerships with Helpers, it is crucial to encourage them to honor their own worth and set clear boundaries. By fostering open dialogue and nurturing their self-care habits, these partnerships can tap into the Helper's natural strengths while ensuring financial stability and prosperity for all involved.

Type 3 individuals, also known as the Achievers, have an innate drive for success and recognition. These individuals bring unparalleled levels of ambition and determination to financial partnerships. With their results-oriented mindset, they excel at setting goals, executing plans, and achieving remarkable financial outcomes.

However, the Achievers' relentless pursuit of external validation can lead to a tendency to prioritize image and outward success over long-term financial stability. It is crucial to help Type 3 individuals strike a balance between their intrinsic drive for achievement and sustainable financial practices. Encouraging them to define success based on their own values, rather than external validation, allows their natural leadership skills and resourcefulness to thrive within partnerships, ensuring both financial triumph and personal fulfillment.

Type 4 individuals, known as the Individualists, contribute a unique and innovative perspective to financial partnerships. These individuals bring a deep sense of authenticity and creativity, which allows for unconventional thinking and presents opportunities for out-of-the-box financial approaches.

However, the Individualists' desire for personal expression and uniqueness may lead to tendencies of financial instability. Their aversion to mundanity and routine can make focusing on practical financial matters challenging. To establish successful financial partnerships with Individualists, it is essential to encourage them to cultivate a balance between creative exploration and practicality. Helping them connect with their inherent value regardless of external circumstances allows their visionary mindset to flourish while ensuring financial stability and abundance.

Type 5 individuals, referred to as the Investigators, possess an insatiable thirst for knowledge and a fiercely independent spirit. These individuals bring exceptional analytical skills and a capacity for deep research that can prove invaluable in financial partnerships.

However, the Investigators' need for autonomy and self-sufficiency can sometimes translate into a reluctance to share their knowledge or collaborate. They may withhold information or remain detached from the financial decision-making process, hindering effective teamwork. To cultivate successful partnerships with Investigators, it is crucial to foster an environment that values their insights and knowledge while encouraging them to embrace collaboration. By striking a balance between independence and collective problem-solving, these partnerships can access the Investigators' intellectual rigor and propel financial endeavors to new heights.

Type 6 individuals, known as the Loyalists, bring a strong sense of loyalty, strategy, and preparedness into financial partnerships. These individuals have an exceptional ability to anticipate potential risks and develop contingency plans, ensuring stability and security in financial ventures.

However, the Loyalists' predisposition towards anxiety and planning can sometimes result in hesitation or overcautiousness. Their fear of making mistakes or encountering unexpected challenges may hinder seizing profitable opportunities. To cultivate successful financial partnerships with Loyalists, it is crucial to foster an environment that balances preparedness with risk-taking. Encouraging open dialogue and providing reassurance can help Loyalists overcome their fears and channel their strategic thinking into ventures that yield substantial financial rewards.

Type 7 individuals, referred to as the Enthusiasts, bring a contagious energy and optimism to financial partnerships. These individuals possess a natural ability to ideate and adapt, making them adept at spotting opportunities and exploring diverse financial avenues.

However, the Enthusiasts' desire for excitement and variety may sometimes lead to a lack of focus or difficulty maintaining long-term financial stability. Their tendency to pursue instant gratification can impede the development of sustainable financial strategies. To foster successful financial partnerships with Enthusiasts, it is essential to help them strike a balance between their desire for exploration and the need for discipline and focus. By guiding them towards setting realistic goals and instilling measures for financial accountability, these partnerships can leverage the Enthusiasts' natural optimism and agility while achieving lasting financial success.

Type 8 individuals, known as the Challengers, bring unwavering assertiveness, integrity, and a desire for control to financial partnerships. These individuals excel at making bold decisions, negotiating favorable terms, and driving financial endeavors forward.

However, the Challengers' assertiveness and need for control can sometimes create challenges within partnerships. Their direct communication style and inclination towards dominance may alienate or overpower others, hindering collaboration. To cultivate successful financial partnerships with Challengers, it is crucial to establish clear communication channels where all voices are heard and respected. Encouraging a healthy balance of power and allowing for flexibility and compromise promotes a strong sense of trust, enabling the Challengers' assertiveness and integrity to thrive within the partnership while ensuring mutual prosperity.

Type 9 individuals, often referred to as the Peacemakers, bring a harmonious and conciliatory spirit to financial partnerships. These individuals possess exceptional mediation skills and the ability to navigate conflicts, fostering a cooperative environment within the partnership.

However, the Peacemakers' desire for peace and harmony may sometimes result in indecisiveness or reluctance to assert their own financial needs. Their accommodating nature can lead to neglecting their own interests or avoiding necessary confrontation. To establish successful financial partnerships with Peacemakers, it is crucial to encourage them to embrace their voice and assert their needs. By cultivating an environment that values open dialogue and encourages active participation, these partnerships can tap into the Peacemakers' natural ability to bring balance and harmony to financial endeavors.

As they delve into the dynamics of Enneagram compatibility in financial partnerships, it becomes evident that no single type can operate in isolation. Achieving remarkable financial success often hinges on the synergy and harmonious collaboration between individuals of different Enneagram types.

By understanding and appreciating the motivations, fears, and strengths of each Enneagram type, they open windows of opportunity for growth and innovation. Collaborating with diverse Enneagram types can foster creativity, challenge assumptions, and drive financial partnerships beyond their perceived limits. However, navigating compatibility can also present its share of challenges. It requires cultivating empathy, understanding, and a willingness to compromise while recognizing and respecting the unique traits and needs of each Enneagram type.

To enhance compatibility in financial relationships, it is vital to maintain open lines of communication, create a safe space for everyone's perspective, and celebrate the diversity of strengths and approaches. By harnessing the collective wisdom of each

Enneagram type, financial partnerships can transcend mediocrity and achieve extraordinary results.

Understanding the dynamics of Enneagram compatibility in financial partnerships is a transformative key to unlocking unprecedented success. Recognizing the distinctive qualities, motivations, and behaviors of each Enneagram type is essential for fostering effective collaboration, overcoming challenges, and maximizing financial outcomes.

Through a deep exploration of the Perfectionist's meticulousness, the Helper's selflessness, the Achiever's ambition, the Individualist's authenticity, the Investigator's thirst for knowledge, the Loyalist's preparedness, the Enthusiast's energy, the Challenger's assertiveness, and the Peacemaker's harmony, financial partnerships can flourish into vibrant ecosystems characterized by resilience, creativity, and abundance.

By embracing the power of Enneagram compatibility and leveraging the diverse strengths offered by each type, they can transcend the limitations of conventional financial collaboration and forge transformative alliances.

As they embark on the next segment, they will explore the profound impact of Enneagram dynamics on personal finance, diving into understanding our own Enneagram type in relation to money, and delving into the transformative practices that align our financial choices with our deepest desires and values.

The Enneagram and Financial Decision-

making

Financial decision-making is a fundamental aspect of our daily lives. From budgeting and investing to saving and spending, our financial choices can have a profound impact on our present and future well-being. However, these decisions are not made in a vacuum. They are influenced by various factors, including our values, beliefs, and personality traits. This is where the Enneagram comes into play.

The Enneagram, a powerful tool for self-awareness and personal growth, can provide valuable insights into our relationship with money. By understanding our Enneagram type and its associated motivations and fears, they can gain a deeper understanding of our financial patterns and behaviors. This self-awareness serves as a foundation for making more informed financial decisions and setting goals for financial growth.

Each Enneagram type has its own unique approach to money and financial decision-making. For example, Type 1 individuals, known as the Perfectionists, may struggle with a perfectionistic approach to money, constantly seeking to make the "right" financial choices. On the other hand, Type 2 individuals, the Helpers, may prioritize the needs of others over their own financial well-being, potentially neglecting their own financial security.

Understanding these tendencies can help us find balance and make more conscious financial choices. For example, Type 3 individuals, the Achievers, may have a natural drive for success and recognition. However, this drive can sometimes lead them to prioritize outward success over long-term financial stability. By defining success based on their own values and priorities, Type 3 individuals can achieve financial fulfillment while staying true to their authentic selves.

Similarly, Type 4 individuals, the Individualists, bring a deep sense of authenticity and creativity to their financial decisions. However, their aversion to routine and practicality can sometimes make it challenging to focus on practical financial matters. Embracing financial stability and abundance while staying true to their unique perspective allows Type 4 individuals to cultivate a healthy and balanced financial life.

Type 5 individuals, the Investigators, possess exceptional analytical skills and a thirst for knowledge. However, their need for autonomy and self-sufficiency can sometimes hinder effective teamwork. By embracing collaboration and finding a balance between independence and collective problem-solving, Type 5 individuals can leverage their intellectual rigor for financial success.

Type 6 individuals, the Loyalists, bring a strong sense of loyalty and preparedness to financial decision-making. However, their anxiety and fear of making mistakes can sometimes prevent them from seizing profitable opportunities. Cultivating financial confidence and resilience, particularly in the face of uncertainty, allows Type 6 individuals to harness their strategic thinking for financial success.

Type 7 individuals, the Enthusiasts, possess a natural ability to ideate and adapt, making them adept at spotting opportunities. However, their desire for excitement and variety can sometimes impede long-term financial stability. By balancing their desire for exploration with discipline and focus, Type 7 individuals can achieve financial fulfillment while maintaining a healthy balance.

Type 8 individuals, the Challengers, bring assertiveness, integrity, and a desire for control to their financial decisions. However, their assertiveness and need for control can sometimes create challenges within partnerships. Striking a healthy balance of power, flexibility, and compromise allows Type 8 individuals to cultivate successful financial partnerships while remaining true to their values.

Finally, Type 9 individuals, the Peacemakers, contribute a harmonious and conciliatory spirit to financial decision-making. However, their desire for peace and harmony can sometimes result in indecisiveness or reluctance to assert their own financial needs. Empowering Type 9 individuals to embrace their voice and assert their needs fosters an environment of open dialogue and collaboration in financial partnerships.

Understanding the dynamics and tendencies of each Enneagram type in financial decision-making allows us to cultivate compatibility in financial partnerships. Collaborating with individuals of different Enneagram types fosters creativity, challenges assumptions, and drives financial endeavors beyond perceived limits. However, it requires cultivating empathy, understanding, and a willingness to compromise while respecting the unique traits and needs of each type.

To enhance compatibility in financial partnerships, maintaining open communication, creating a safe space for diverse perspectives, and celebrating the strengths of each Enneagram type are essential. By harnessing the collective wisdom of each type, financial partnerships can transcend mediocrity and achieve extraordinary results.

The Enneagram's role in financial decision-making is a transformative key to unlocking unprecedented success. By recognizing and understanding the motivations, fears, and strengths of each Enneagram type, they can foster effective collaboration, overcome challenges, and maximize financial outcomes. Through a deep exploration of the Perfectionist's meticulousness, the Helper's selflessness, the Achiever's ambition, the Individualist's authenticity, the Investigator's thirst for knowledge, the Loyalist's preparedness, the Enthusiast's energy, the Challenger's assertiveness, and the Peacemaker's harmony, financial partnerships can flourish into vibrant ecosystems characterized by resilience, creativity, and abundance.

Financial Healing Through the Enneagram

The concept of financial healing through the Enneagram is a fascinating exploration of the deep connections between our personalities, motivations, and our relationship with money. As a finance expert with a keen interest in the Enneagram,

I have witnessed firsthand the transformative power of this system in the realm of finance. The Enneagram offers a pathway for personal growth and transformation, allowing us to uncover and heal deep-seated beliefs and patterns that impact our financial behaviors. Through the Enneagram, they can cultivate greater self-awareness, break free from limiting financial patterns, align our values and actions, and foster financial well-being as a holistic state. By diving deep into the Enneagram's insights, they can tap into a profound journey of financial healing and discover the keys to unlocking our true financial potential.

At the core of financial healing through the Enneagram is the recognition that our financial behaviors are deeply rooted in our personalities and motivations. The Enneagram reveals our core fears, desires, defense mechanisms, and unconscious patterns related to money. By understanding these underlying factors, they can begin to untangle the web of emotions, beliefs, and behaviors that shape our financial reality. This self-awareness offers a powerful pathway for transformation, as it allows us to identify and address unhealthy money behaviors and beliefs that may be holding us back from financial growth and well-being.

To embark on this journey of financial healing through the Enneagram, it is essential to explore the nine distinct Enneagram types and their unique perspectives on money. Each type has its own financial mindset and behaviors, shaped by their core motivations and fears. The Perfectionist, for example, tends to be meticulous and detail-oriented in financial matters, seeking security and control. The Helper, on the other hand, may prioritize the needs of others over their own and struggle with setting boundaries in financial relationships. The Achiever is driven by a desire for success, often working tirelessly to attain financial recognition and status. The Individualist seeks authenticity and personal expression in their finances, often defying societal norms. The Investigator, with their analytical skills, thirsts for knowledge and understanding of financial systems. The Loyalist brings loyalty and preparedness to financial decision-making, but may struggle with anxiety and fear of making mistakes. The Enthusiast is prone to seek excitement and variety in financial endeavors, sometimes sacrificing long-term stability. The Challenger, driven by a need for power and control, may need to find a balance between assertiveness and allowing space for others in financial partnerships. Finally, the Peacemaker strives for harmony and may avoid conflict or assertiveness in financial settings. These descriptions provide a foundation for later chapters that delve deeper into each type's financial mindset and offer strategies for growth and balance.

One of the most transformative aspects of the Enneagram's role in financial healing is its ability to help us break free from limiting patterns and beliefs. By becoming aware of our Enneagram type, they gain insight into the underlying motivations and fears that drive our financial behaviors. This awareness empowers us to identify and challenge the unhealthy patterns that may be holding us back from financial growth and well-being. Through the Enneagram, they can develop new, healthier habits and beliefs that support our financial goals and align with our true selves.

Financial well-being, as a holistic state, goes beyond mere monetary success. It involves aligning our values, goals, and actions with our Enneagram type's natural strengths and growth areas. By understanding our type-specific tendencies and challenges, they can consciously work towards creating a harmonious relationship with money. This may involve embracing an abundance mindset, shifting our perspectives on scarcity, and cultivating gratitude and generosity in our financial lives. The Enneagram provides valuable insights into our relationship with abundance and scarcity, revealing how different types tend to have different associations and attitudes towards money, which impact their financial well-being. By harnessing these insights, they can develop strategies and practices that promote financial abundance and well-being.

A key aspect of financial healing through the Enneagram is its focus on uncovering and addressing the emotional and psychological factors that contribute to our financial challenges. The Enneagram's deep exploration of motivation and core fears allows us to bring awareness to the underlying emotional and psychological patterns that shape our financial behaviors. By understanding the root causes of our financial challenges, they can work towards healing and transformation in this area of our lives. This may involve techniques such as self-reflection, journaling, meditation, and seeking support from professionals or mentors who can guide us on our financial healing journey.

In our pursuit of financial healing through the Enneagram, it is vital to cultivate self-acceptance and self-compassion. Understanding our Enneagram type allows us to embrace our unique strengths and challenges without judgment. This self-acceptance opens the door to a more balanced and compassionate approach to our financial well-being. Rather than striving for an idealized version of financial success, they can learn to appreciate and work with our individual financial strengths. By nurturing self-compassion, they can forgive themselves for past mistakes, release shame and guilt, and move forward with clarity and confidence.

To support our financial healing journey through the Enneagram, there are specific practices and exercises tailored to each Enneagram type's needs. These practices vary from journaling prompts and self-reflection exercises to meditation techniques that help us cultivate awareness and mindfulness in our financial decisions. By engaging in these practices regularly, they deepen our understanding of our unique financial patterns and beliefs, and work towards transformation and growth in this area of our lives.

Financial healing through the Enneagram is an ongoing process. It requires continued self-reflection, self-awareness, and growth to maintain and deepen our financial well-being. The Enneagram offers a wealth of resources and recommendations for further exploration and support on this journey. Books, workshops, online courses, and Enneagram communities provide avenues for continued learning and growth. Engaging in ongoing self-reflection and seeking support from professionals or mentors can also be instrumental in sustaining our financial healing.

As they conclude this segment of the book, they transition to the next chapter, which delves into the specific financial mindset and behaviors of Type 1 individuals. they will explore the unique challenges and growth opportunities for Type 1s and offer strategies for their financial growth and balance. Through this exploration, they continue our journey of financial healing through the Enneagram, guided by the understanding that our personalities shape our financial realities, and that deep self-awareness and transformation can lead us to financial well-being aligned with our true selves.

Our exploration of the Enneagram and its relationship with money has provided valuable insights into the connection between our unique personalities and our financial patterns and behaviors. By understanding our Enneagram type, they can uncover deep-seated beliefs and unconscious patterns that influence our financial decisions.

We have delved into the financial mindset and behaviors of each Enneagram type, from the Perfectionist's pursuit of financial perfection to the Peacemaker's desire for financial harmony. They have discussed the challenges faced by each type, as well as the pathways to financial growth and balance that are specific to their needs and motivations.

Throughout this book, we have seen how the Enneagram can serve as a roadmap for financial transformation. It has provided us with a deeper understanding of ourselves and our tendencies when it comes to money. Through this awareness, they can break free from unhealthy patterns and make conscious choices that align with our values and financial goals.

It is important to note that the Enneagram is not a static system. They are constantly evolving and growing, and our financial behaviors are no exception. The insights gained from this book are just the beginning of our journey towards financial empowerment and fulfillment.

It is my hope that this book has sparked a curiosity and desire for further exploration. The Enneagram is a rich and multifaceted tool that can be applied to many areas of our lives, including our finances. With each passing day, new resources and experts emerge, offering fresh perspectives and expanding our understanding of the Enneagram's impact on our financial lives.

I encourage you, dear reader, to take the knowledge and insights gained from this book and apply them to your own financial journey. Take the time to reflect on your Enneagram type and consider how it influences your relationship with money. Use this understanding to make intentional choices and set meaningful goals that align with your true self.

Remember, the Enneagram is a powerful tool, but it is only as effective as our willingness to engage with it. Embrace a mindset of continuous learning and growth, seek out new resources, attend workshops or conferences, and connect with like-minded individuals. Surround yourself with a supportive community that can provide guidance, accountability, and inspiration as you navigate your financial path.

In closing, I express my deepest gratitude to you, the reader, for embarking on this journey with me. Your engagement and willingness to explore the connection between the Enneagram and money is a testament to your commitment to personal and financial growth. May your continued exploration of the Enneagram lead you to a life of financial abundance, alignment, and authenticity.

Don't miss out!

Visit the website below and you can sign up to receive emails whenever Bradley Hall publishes a new book. There's no charge and no obligation.

https://books2read.com/r/B-A-SCSZ-MYQNC

BOOKS 2 READ

Connecting independent readers to independent writers.